Willa Cather's
Sexual Aesthetics
and the
Male Homosexual
Literary Tradition

WILLA CATHER'S

SEXUAL

AESTHETICS

and the MALE

HOMOSEXUAL

LITERARY

TRADITION

John P. Anders

University of

Nebraska Press

LINCOLN

& LONDON

(∞)

Library of Congress Cataloging-in-Publication Data
Anders, John P., 1948–
    Willa Cather's sexual aesthetics and the male homosexual
literary tradition / John P. Anders.
        p.   cm.
    Includes bibliographical references (p.   ) and index.
    ISBN 0-8032-1053-1 (cloth : alk. paper)
    1. Cather, Willa, 1873–1947—Characters—Men. 2. Homo-
sexuality and literature—United States—History—20th century.
3. Influence (Literary, artistic, etc.) 4. Male friendship in literature. 5. Gay men in literature. 6. Aesthetics, American.
7. Men in literature. 8. Sex in literature. I. Title.
PS3505.A87Z557   1999
813'.52—dc21   99-10701
                                                           CIP

Only the feeling matters.
Willa Cather, *One of Ours*

In memory of my grandmother
"think not I forget"

Contents

Preface

In a recent study of Willa Cather, Edward Wagenknecht asks if Cather "ever took up any attitude toward homosexuality as a phenomenon?" (160). This is a timely and important question yet one that Wagenknecht and I answer differently. "I have found," he states, "little or nothing except for her comments on the Oscar Wilde case in the 1890s, which are little short of savage" (160).

Surely by now, gay and lesbian studies have made deep enough inroads into Cather scholarship to dispel such conclusions. Even Cather's response to Oscar Wilde, I believe, is more ambivalent than Wagenknecht allows. For instance, although scathing in her newspaper articles, Cather is surprisingly sympathetic toward Wilde in her fiction. The same can be said of her attitude toward Walt Whitman. Indeed, from her earliest stories through her major novels and up to her last unfinished and unpublished fragment, the phenomenon of homosexuality makes itself felt in Cather's narratives. Likewise, both her first critical statements and her later essays all reveal its impact upon her imagination.

Foremost is the connection between a homosexual sensibility and Cather's feelings about art. Just as Harold Bloom praises Cather for her "aesthetic eminence" (436) in the twentieth century, I argue that her artistic achievements are further distinguished by her "sexual aesthetics," an elusive (and allusive) literary style inextricably associated with homosexuality. But rather than challenging traditional Cather criticism, I seek to go beyond it, drawing from it while at the same time leading it in new directions. "Let us hope at least," Wagenknecht concludes, "that whatever she believed, there was some advance in the direction of Christian charity" (160). Here he and I agree, for the very nature of Cather's aesthetics encourages a wide play of human feelings, a creative interplay between Cather's gift of sympathy and her sympathetic imagination.

Although Willa Cather is primarily known for creating strong, female characters, more often than not her fiction centers in male friendships, evident throughout her career but especially present in her novels of the 1920s. Not surprisingly, this persistent focus leads to homosexual interpretations of her work. And while no text in Cather's canon benefits more from a gay reading than *One of Ours*, her Pulitzer Prize–winning novel of World War I, similar readings of other texts further demonstrate the value of such revisioning. Male friendship, of course, is not necessarily gay, or homosexual, or even homoerotic. Yet neither is it necessarily the opposite. Rather, male friendships, like friendship in general, exist along a continuum from the social to the sexual. In Cather's works, some friendships seem fixed, closer to the social end of the spectrum than to the sexual or erotic, while others are more fluid, oscillating between homosocial and homosexual experience.

This study examines such patterns of friendship in Cather's fiction and their contribution to her art. The analysis here is, I like to think, a dialogue of sorts—a bridge, perhaps, between Cather studies and gay studies. Intended as a work of advocacy, it is not meant to be sexual politics; I emphasize instead a new aestheticism. And while it would be difficult to write about an author's work without exploring to some extent that author's life, this is not a critical biography. Any discussion of Cather's life would invoke her lesbianism, but the aesthetics about which I speak are of male homosexuality. Consequently, it is that literary tradition I examine, for it—more than any other—shaped Cather's writing. In considering the range and potential of this influence, I tend to use words like *homosexual, homosexuality, homoerotic, homoeroticism,* and *gay* interchangeably. To do otherwise, to be unduly precise, would defeat the purpose of this book and, I believe, of Cather's books as well.

In chapter 1, I present the argument for a gay reading of Cather's texts. Next, I discuss the homosexual literary traditions available to Cather. In chapter 3, I locate intimations of homosexuality in Cather's early fiction. In the three succeeding chapters, I interpret the later, male-centered novels—*One of Ours* (1922), *The Professor's House* (1926), and *Death Comes for the Archbishop* (1927)—from the perspective of a specifically homosexual paradigm. I conclude by designating Cather a writer of gay fiction. Throughout, my methodology aims to verify Wayne Koestenbaum's assertion that "gay criticism can illuminate Wordsworth as well as Wilde" (DT 5). My hope is to show that this critical approach will also illuminate Willa Cather.

Apart from all this, these chapters indirectly address another question: what is it that attracts a gay reader to the works of Willa Cather? Again, Koestenbaum offers a clue to the mystery, acknowledging that "a gay criticism that cooperates with its own desires will be able to find meanings that would, to other readers, remain invisible" (DT 7). More than any other writer I know, Willa Cather invites such intimacy.

• • •

I would like to thank the University of Nebraska Press for its interest in this project and my friends in the Cather community for their generous support and encouragement. I also wish to thank Gayle Swanson for copyediting and Sarah Fairchild and Julie Thomson for creating the index.

Some parts of this book are revisions of essays that have appeared previously. The "French" section of chapter 2 was pub-

lished as "Willa Cather, France, and Pierre Loti: A Spirit of Affiliation," *Willa Cather Pioneer Memorial Newsletter* 38 (winter 1995):
15–18. Chapter 6 will appear as "'Something Soft and Wild and
Free': Willa Cather's Sexual Aesthetics," in *Cather Studies 4: Willa
Cather's Canadian and Old World Connections,* ed. Robert Thacker
and Michael Peterman (Lincoln: University of Nebraska Press,
1999).

1

"The Thing Not Named"

WHEN Willa Cather wrote in *One of Ours* that "Only the feeling matters" (329), she was reaffirming in her fiction what had become the touchstone of her art. Appearing the same year that novel was published, Cather's essay "The Novel Démeublé" again articulated her literary ideals: "Whatever is felt upon the page without being specifically named there—that, one might say, is created. It is the inexplicable presence of the thing not named, of the overtone divined by the ear but not heard by it, the verbal mood, the emotional aura of the fact or the thing or the deed, that gives high quality to the novel or the drama, as well as to poetry itself" (50). Together these two statements clarify Cather's artistic philosophy, her belief in literature as an intensely subjective experience dually created by the writer and reader. Whether in fiction or prose, in theory or practice, no single idea more fully encompasses all that Willa Cather is about.

One aspect of Cather's fiction that evokes strong feelings is its concern for friendship. As readers and critics have long recognized, Cather finds positive value in friendship and constantly seeks ways to convey its potential. For example, both *My Ántonia* and its dedication to Carrie and Irene Miner "In memory of affections old and true" acknowledge a connection between childhood friendship and creativity. Friendships with men also shaped Cather's imagination, whether family members and early mentors or business associates like S. S. McClure and Alfred Knopf. Considering friendship necessary in marriage, Cather writes in *O Pioneers!* that "when friends marry, they are safe" (308). And regarding friendships between women, James Woodress maintains that "Cather derived her greatest comfort, pleasure, moral support, and satisfaction from friendships with members of her own sex" ("Cather and Her Friends" 94). Cather's lifelong relationship with Edith Lewis attests to the importance she placed upon such commitments and helps explain her emotional ties with other women, including Isabelle McClung, for whom Cather felt "all her books had been written" (Woodress, LL 139).

Cather's biography, however, cannot always account for the rendering of friendship in her fiction, where the values she associates with friendship in her own life are most often explored within all-male relationships. Male protagonists like Claude Wheeler, Godfrey St. Peter, and Jean Latour experience emotional intimacy with other men during their lives, and these friendships create compelling models of human happiness. In addition to this central position, male friendships also occupy the background of much of Cather's fiction.

Friendships between men strike many readers as a curious departure from Cather's personal experience. Her literary style adds to this confusion. Critics emphasize Cather's tendency to tease, pointing out as has Janis Stout that "Again and again she brings the alert reader to the point of asking, but does not raise the question directly or, of course, provide an answer" (85). Nowhere is a reader more bewildered than in determining the exact nature of Cather's all-male relationships. Are they strictly friendship, or does Cather imply something else? If friendship alone, is Cather working within the familiar tradition of friendship literature inspired by classical and Christian texts and sanctioned throughout history; if more than friendship, is she borrowing from another body of literature, a homosexual legacy that is part of yet distinctly apart from established literary traditions? Or does Cather possibly combine the two, thus giving her fiction an unexpected depth and complexity while adding another layer of ambiguity to her art?

Homosexuality can be felt throughout Cather's fiction, whether as a dimension of friendship, delineated within a single character, or implicit in the narrative voice. But to sense homosexuality is one thing; to demonstrate its existence is quite another. Distrusting analysis of any kind, Cather places her faith in the suggestiveness of art and endorses a creative response to its subjective power. Her critical signpost is once again clear: "the facts are nothing, the feeling is everything" (Cather, "Defoe's *The Fortunate Mistress*" 84).

Critics have begun to turn their feelings about homosexuality in Cather's fiction into provocative interpretations. Sharon O'Brien perhaps first opened interpretative doors by drawing attention to similarities between Cather's elusive poetics and the erotic dictum associated with Oscar Wilde:

> In her often-quoted essay on the craft of fiction, "The Novel Démeublé," Willa Cather asks her readers to consider the importance of an unnamed, absent presence in the literary text. Whereas phrases like "overtone," "verbal mood," and "emotional aura" suggest ineffable realms of experience and feeling—complex or barely sensed signifieds for which there exists no precise verbal signifier—Cather's startling phrase "the thing not named" has another connotation: an aspect of experience possessing a name that the writer does not, or cannot, employ. A sophisticated novelist well read in fin de siècle literature, Cather must have been aware of the similarity between the phrase she made central to her literary aesthetic and the phrase used as evidence in Oscar Wilde's trial: "the Love that dared not speak its name." ("'The Thing Not Named'" 576–77)

"The thing not named" may be Cather's lesbianism, as O'Brien persuasively argues, but, ironically, the impulse is felt in her work as male homosexuality. Explanations of this transformation often suggest that Cather was unable to write of the realities of her life

directly, so she did so indirectly by turning male friendship into a
mask for love between women. Doris Grumbach, for instance,
generalizes that all Cather's male pairs are really disguised female
pairs, a coded strategy of gender duplicity by which Cather could
explore the central truth of her life without fear of social exposure
("Just William" 24). Although a reluctance to portray female
friendships in a society increasingly insensitive, suspicious, and
hostile concerning same-sex relationships is understandable, this
explanation does not sufficiently account either for why Cather
chose to write of male relationships instead or, more especially, for
her willingness to invest these relationships with sexual overtones.[1]

While sympathetic to the dilemma, such arguments subvert
Cather's texts with tantalizing alternatives, a practice that critics
like Hermione Lee emphatically reject:

> To account for Cather's fiction by reading it as an encoding of cov-
> ert, even guilty, sexuality, is, I think, patronizing and narrow. It as-
> sumes that the work is written only in order to express homosexual
> feelings in disguise; it makes her out to be a coward (which was cer-
> tainly not one of her failings); and it assumes that 'openness' would
> have been preferable. If the argument is that 'Cather never dealt
> adequately with her homosexuality in her fiction,' that *My Ántonia*
> is 'a betrayal of female independence and female sexuality,' and that
> *The Professor's House* and *Death Comes for the Archbishop* retreat into
> 'a world dominated by patriarchy,' then Cather is diminished by
> being enlisted to a cause. She was a writer who worked, at her best,
> through indirection, suppression, and suggestion, and through a
> refusal to be enlisted. (11–12)

Similar views emphasize the ability of the writer to transcend the
limitations of self, gender, and sexuality in the creative process
(O'Brien, "'The Thing Not Named'" 599); to question that ability
is to question the autonomy of art and the artist.

Now seems to be the appropriate time to ask other questions of
Cather's fiction. Although she wrote about women and female experience, Cather also wrote about men, yet critical analysis often

overlooks her presentation of their lives. Susan J. Rosowski ad-
dresses this neglect:

> We have become sensitive to ways in which Cather broke through
> hidebound conventions regarding women, yet generalizations
> about Cather's male characters remain largely unexamined. Cather
> created weak men, we are told, because they are often supportive,
> reflective, sensitive, poetic, emotional, onlookers rather than at the
> center of the action. Most damning, they are often eclipsed by pow-
> erful women. Nowhere does Cather evoke questions about those
> assumptions more powerfully than in *One of Ours*, but her explora-
> tion of effects of gender conventions upon men extends through
> her writing. (VP 112–13)

Rather than creating weak men, Cather creates revisionary texts on
manhood. Even more radical is her method, for the same qualities
Cather attributes to her central male characters are those frequently used by society to stereotype homosexuals. By evoking
homosexuality to reenvision a masculine ideal, Cather creates fiction that is revolutionary indeed.

What did Cather know of men's lives, and what were her strategies for writing about them? The juncture of gender studies and
gay studies provides a lens through which to explore these questions. Gender studies encourages a revisionist reading of literature
with an increased awareness of instances when male characters
break out of the confines of stereotypical masculine behavior
(Reimer 298). Gay studies complements this search as it attempts
to give greater visibility to issues previously ignored or margin-
alized. Cather creates particularized men coming to terms with
gender identity, and for her, homosexuality becomes an innovative
strategy to reflect this process. When the sexual implications of
men engaged in intimacy are critically addressed, readers are less
likely to gloss the complexities of Cather's male relationships. At
the same time, it shifts attention from a narrow focus on Cather's
personal sexuality and illuminates her transcendence, thereby underscoring Jane Rule's admonition that "No novel by a writer of

real gifts should be read as veiled autobiography" (85). Consequently, studies of male homosexuality in Cather's fiction are usually concerned less with the range of her experience than with the reach of her art.

In addition to its Wildean overtones, the language of Cather's poetics closely resembles sexual discourse. Throughout her critical statements, erotically charged words like "urge," "drive," "passion," and "desire" imply parallels between sex and art and suffuse Cather's aesthetics with the pressure of sexuality. Critics underscore the significance of this intonation. For instance, Edward A. and Lillian D. Bloom write that for Cather the artist's primary motivation is "a desire for self-expression so individually compelling that it must find its natural outlet" (174), and they emphasize that great art "is compulsive in its need for release" (200). While biographical studies suggest that writing was the transcendent experience in which Cather found fulfillment and that she "was married to her art" (Woodress, LL 125), a sexual urgency nonetheless invigorates her creative desire.

While an eroticized poetics lifts Cather's discussion of art into a sexual realm, the emotional resonance of her language lends itself to a specifically homosexual eros. The late-nineteenth-century notion of the artist as homosexual and, conversely, of the homosexual as artist is a measure of Oscar Wilde's contribution to the aesthetic movement. During this period, homosexual sentiments were accepted "as part of the whole range of feeling which waited to be explored" and "grew into a belief that the more acute sensibility of the 'artistic temperament' was often allied to the frustrated senses of the homosexual. To be homosexually inclined thus became one of the secondary qualifications for declaring oneself an 'artist'" (Reade 31). The romantic ideology of the artist as a solitary figure strengthens this parallel as the estrangement of the artist from an unsympathetic public mirrors the estrangement of the homosexual from a hostile society. The Blooms comment that "Throughout her life Miss Cather was intrigued by the image of the artist and the need to portray him" and would find "kindred motivations" between the artist and her priests and pioneers (117). The image of the artist as a homosexual adds depth to Cather's portrayals and endows her protagonists with ambiguous feelings and complex, often frustrated, desires.

Definitions of homosexual art further support this affiliation. Robert K. Martin generalizes that "Gay literature has always, since the Greeks, been a literature of indirection" (HT 219). Stressing the tension between repression and expression, Jeffrey Meyers further distinguishes gay novels as "characteristically subtle, allusive and symbolic—the very qualities we now admire in the poetry of Yeats and Eliot, and the novels of Flaubert and Henry James—and form an eighth kind of literary ambiguity" (1). Oscillating between disclosure and concealment, Cather's fiction follows this literary pattern, and the presence of "the thing not named" echoes both Oscar Wilde and the cultural climate he inspired.[2]

The reading of textual silences intensifies discussions of homosexuality in Cather's art.[3] Without this critical inquiry such possibilities have remained latent, a silencing ironically illustrated by the exclusion of Cather from early bibliographies of gay literature. For example, in *The Male Homosexual in Literature* Ian Young focuses on fiction dealing explicitly with homosexuality or having gay-identified characters. Similarly, in *The Gay Novel* James Levin limits his discussion to novels in which overt homosexual behavior is a central theme. Implicit in these restrictions is the notion of what constitutes a "novel," and in the case of Levin, his narrow, realistic definition is at odds with Cather's elusive statements on the art of fiction. Definitions of gay novels are also circumscribed by definitions of homosexuality itself, ranging, as Rictor Norton points out, from "the exclusively sexual penetration of one male by another" to "the ambiguously intermingled erotic, emotional, and spiritual relationship between members of the same sex" ("Ganymede Raped" 201). Indicative of the short-sightedness of reductive criteria is Levin's assertion that "there is no American male homosexual novel in the 1920's" (31), the decade of Cather's most intense explorations of male friendship. Overt homosexual acts are no more present in Cather's fiction than are overt heterosexual acts, yet Cather would certainly know that descriptions of emotional intimacy between men would encourage homosexual interpretations of her work. Consequently, when she celebrates male friendships, she implicitly acknowledges their connotations as well. While bibliographies like Levin's and Young's have provided a valuable foundation for gay studies, new definitions of gay literature that can accommodate sexual ambiguity are needed. Roger Austen makes this effort in *Playing the Game;* and in *Gay Fictions* Claude J. Summers includes Cather among the authors who have shaped modern homosexual literature.

Part of the difficulty in attempting to place Cather within this tradition is finding appropriate terminology to describe the canon itself, a word or words suggestive enough to include all such literature yet limited enough to have specific meaning. Addressing this daunting task, Norton catalogs the baffling consequences of attempting a too-inclusive definition of gay literature: "Before one knows what's happening," he warns, *"the entire western literary tradition will be subsumed by the homosexual literary tradition"* ("Ganymede Raped" 201).[4] By redefining lesbianism to include emotional attachments between women, feminist critics have inadvertently offered a possible solution to this rhetorical impasse. Woodress considers its impact upon Cather: "If one defines a lesbian as a woman who has sexual relations with another woman, Cather cannot be called a lesbian on the basis of available records. On the other hand, if a lesbian is a woman whose primary emotional attachments are to other women, regardless of sexual relations, the definition adopted by some feminists, then Cather was most certainly a lesbian" (LL 141). If lesbianism needs to be redefined in the effort to understand Cather's personal life, then homosexuality likewise needs redefining for us to understand her fiction. The word *gay*, I feel, brings us closer to such a redefinition because it can include an emotional identity regardless of its physical expression. By questioning the assumption that it is not homosexual unless genital activity occurs, such flexible terminology radically alters definitions of homosexual experience. Thus when I use terms like *gay* and *homosexual*, I mean them in their broadest, most overlapping sense, incorporating all aspects of same-sex love and eroticism and their accompanying phenomena.

While critics have long attempted to explain the motives behind Cather's silences and to determine the source of her reticence, affinities between Cather's aesthetics and a homosexual sensibility raise new questions about her art. Did Cather's subject determine her style, or did her preferred method find its appropriate material? Put another way, is homosexuality Cather's strategy, or is it her subject, or is it a fusion of the two? Given her eroticized poetics, the application of a sexual paradigm to explore such questions seems promising. Although Cather eschewed depicting "physical sensations" ("The Novel Démeublé" 50), sexuality suffuses her work to the extent that her reticence becomes less a disavowal of physiology than a discreet challenge of sexual norms; placing homosexuality in a reader's mind further inscribes that challenge by calling into question ideas about gender, culture, identity, and desire.[5]

Gay parallels become clearer when such connections are made. Silenced by a prohibitive culture, the phenomenon of homosexuality—"the love that dared not speak its name"—helped Cather develop a sensitivity to human variation and a style to accommodate it. The range of male friendship and masculine desire in Cather's fiction demonstrates this gift of sympathy and registers its sincerity. But while Cather's wide play of feelings opened to her the imaginative possibilities of human differences, homosexuality does more than humanize her fiction; it transmutes that humanity into art. I would argue further that while the subject of homosexuality enables Cather to refine her characteristically subtle and elusive style, it becomes in effect the objective correlative of her art, dramatizing the diversity of human nature as it simultaneously deepens the mystery of her texts.

Such a claim for the place of homosexuality in Cather's fiction increases our understanding of her development, for while she extends the literary tradition of homosexuality, that tradition in turn extends her art. In the prefatory note to *Not Under Forty* Cather claims to be among the "backward" goers. But at times she is distinctly modern, and critics are now beginning to recognize her modernist tendencies. Jo Ann Middleton defines modernism as "the outlook that views the world in its complexity, refuses to accept single or conventional solutions, and then experiments with new answers and radical suggestions" (10). Cather's treatment of homosexuality is one means by which to assess not only her ties with the past but the experimental nature of her fiction as well, for homosexuality, while timeless, is a persistently modern concern, emblematic of everything from sin and salvation to happiness and despair. Coincidentally, Cather's initial exclusion from gay bibliographies recalls her similar dismissal by the avant-garde: "First, Cather's work appeared too simple and clear, too easily understood; complexity was integral to the modernists. Second, they must have believed that Cather was too popular a writer to be very good; a certain elitism marked the new breed of writer. Third, Cather's subject matter seemed nostalgic, her style seemed romantic, and her respect for tradition seemed old-fashioned to those revolting against nineteenth-century literary conventions" (Middleton 37).

An aura of homosexuality reinforces Cather's modernism. Austen charts the 1920s as a time when "the American mentality was so wised-up that the camouflaged approach of *Joseph and His Friend* [Bayard Taylor, 1870] and *South-Sea Idyls* [Charles Warren Stoddard, 1873] would no longer work, but at the same time it remained so homophobic that *The Well of Loneliness* [Radclyffe Hall, 1928] was judged to be obscene" (PG 35). Freudian self-consciousness about sex and sexuality had also entered American minds, and what had once been seen as effusive sentiment was now viewed as sublimated desire. While Cather looks back to inherited homosexual traditions that idealize male friendship, she brings those traditions into the twentieth century with its accompanying awareness of deviancy and perversion, thus placing herself on a literary continuum from Plato to Proust. As a result, many of the qualities that make Cather's writing compelling literature also make it compelling gay fiction.[6]

Homosexuality also heightens Cather's romanticism. "Romance," in Bernice Slote's words, "exalts courage, honor, daring, love, and all the emotions she considered ennobling; it also represents the creative, exploring truth of the imagination" ("First Principles" 63). Rejecting homosexual realism as she did realism in general, Cather develops instead its potential for romantic affirmation. In *Homosexuality: The Psychology of the Creative Process*, Paul Rosenfels examines this foundation of homosexuality. "The more the individual develops his love capacities in a creative direction," he writes, "the less likely it is that he will be able to accept the external prohibitions established by social institutions" (15). Gay fiction explores this psychological truth as its protagonists often struggle for personal meaning and self-expression in the face of social hostility. Consequently, the romantic quest becomes a modernist quest, verifying Rosowski's observation that "the Romantics inaugurated modern literature" (VP x). And while Leslie Fiedler finds homoeroticism prevalent in American romanticism, Ian Young goes further to say that modern gay fiction is "among the last remaining examples of Romantic literature" ("The Flower" 160). "For the homosexual," Young writes, "there has been no accepted course of behavior, no rules or guidelines for his or her life to follow, and the condition of existential freedom in which he finds himself is central to contemporary philosophic and social concerns: alienation, individualism vs. social conformity, the interplay between value and act, the worth of personal relationships, the meaning of sex, and, not least, the nature of love" (160–61). Placed in this context, homosexuality offers Cather a potent means for exploring her lifelong commitment to romanticism. But whether Cather is seen as a classicist, a romantic, or a modernist, or any amalgam of the three, the dynamics between her subject and her style enliven her art and shape our perceptions of it.

If homosexuality remains unnamed in Cather's texts, how does she make a reader feel its presence? Indeed, how does one attempt to objectify what is subjectively rendered? While I do not propose to solve Cather's enigma, exploring her aesthetics can heighten our experience of it. To create an "awakening of the spirit" (Cather, W&P 371), Cather renounces specificity and encourages creative interplay with her texts through a language of possibility. Repetition of the word "something" exemplifies her skill, and the ways it has been interpreted verify her success. Evading precise definition, the word teases a reader much like Cather's heroines elude her narrators or her novels resist interpretation. Cather uses "something" so often that it becomes a motif, engendering feelings of mystery and awe. Although it is perhaps unlikely that the cryptic word "something" is a coded reference just for homosexuality, by conflating indeterminacy of meaning and sexual ambiguity, Cather positions it beside other possibilities.[7] As human nature is different, so too can a writer choose different strategies to portray its variety. Homosexuality hovers above Cather's narratives and insistently lingers behind their veiled essence. She hints at it early in her writing, incorporates it into her aesthetics, and increasingly realizes its technical and thematic potential.

Cather's treatment of homosexuality presents engaging interpretative questions. How close does she come to her homosexual sources, and does the term "gay fiction" apply to her art? Rather than enlisting Cather in a cause, I wish to place her fiction in a rich literary tradition and study their interaction. Broader contexts, hopefully, will open her work to wider discussion. Although Cather does not write explicitly homosexual fiction, she does employ aspects of homosexuality in her writing. Does that make it gay fiction? I would answer yes, corroborating my feeling with Gregory Woods's definition of a gay text as "one which lends itself to the hypothesis of a gay reading" (4). Certainly Cather's texts so render themselves: homosexual feelings, not homosexual facts, pervade her art.

As Cather's reputation grows, so too does interest in all aspects of her work. Both our understanding and appreciation are possibly diminished without an awareness of her sexual aesthetics. While "Paul's Case" is the story most often selected as Cather's representative gay fiction, it is also the story that signals the end of her apprenticeship, thus drawing attention to the correlation between homosexuality and the development of her art. But if "Paul's Case" signifies Cather's personal and artistic growth, what works mark her subsequent development, and what role does homosexuality play in that maturation?

My focus in Cather is not so much on homosexual definition as it is on how homosexuality defines her art. The questions I have been posing throughout this introductory chapter are those I address in the following chapters. My purpose is not to isolate or insist upon this approach but, rather, to integrate it with traditional interpretations. Cather scholarship is, I believe, ready to accommodate such a thesis, and the results may be surprisingly salutary. For in extending Cather's gift of sympathy, we expand our own and come close to the sensitive readers she envisioned, who, like the writer herself, bring to a work imaginative excitement and take from it the joy of literary creation.

2

Gay Literary
Traditions

In *Willa Cather: A Literary Life* James Woodress emphasizes that "Cather always wrote with an awareness of her literary predecessors from the Greeks to the major authors of the twentieth century" (247). A homosexual tradition lies within that spectrum, and Cather's familiarity with it also seems particularly acute. Although efforts to place Cather in a mainstream literary tradition often overlook "nontraditional" influences, attention to gay texts significantly broadens her literary inheritance, and the homosexual tradition, coming of age as Cather herself came of age, provides a rich context for exploring her fiction. Rather than attempting a comprehensive survey of that tradition, I will seek places where Cather and gay literature connect, guided throughout by what Richard Dellamora describes as a "spirit of affiliation" (218).

For Cather, declares Bernice Slote, "books and reading were among the most personal and necessary things in her life" ("First Principles" 37) and constituted "the stream of experience most central to her own creativity" (35). A list of the books Cather read as a child includes the Bible; *Pilgrim's Progress;* the epics of Homer and Virgil; histories of Alexander, Rome, and the Spanish explorers; Shakespeare; and *The Arabian Nights* (Slote, "First Principles" 35–36). During her college years Cather's reading shifted to essays and novels, especially the hardy romances, or "boys' books" (Cather, KA 337), of Rudyard Kipling, Robert Louis Stevenson, and Alexandre Dumas *père*. About these selections Sharon O'Brien notices that "all were stories of heroes who exercised courage, physical prowess, and daring in overcoming obstacles. Although they represented various genres and national literatures, such narratives exhibited the self-reliance she found in Emerson, her favorite prose writer, who encouraged all readers of 'Nature' to go forth and build their own worlds" (EV 82). Intricately connected with these choices is Cather's attitude toward reading itself, an intimate engagement with books that allowed her to imaginatively participate in their creation.

This brief outline provides a useful background for considering Cather's responsiveness to gay texts. Whatever led Cather to write about homosexuality—whether her lesbianism, her sympathy, or her artistry—creative reading gave her the authority to do so convincingly. Trusting literature to provide truth, Cather gained insights into homosexual experience from extensive reading, and she draws upon this knowledge throughout her fiction.

Which texts, then, that are part of the gay literary heritage were available to Cather, and what was her reaction to them? While Cather never made a list of famous homosexual authors or wrote a "cause célèbre" or a "succès de scandale" or privately printed or left unpublished a work on a "forbidden" subject, as did some of her contemporaries, her literary criticism is one measure of her connection with the homosexual tradition. Working as a journalist during her years as a student at the University of Nebraska and afterwards in Pittsburgh and New York, until her resignation from *McClure's Magazine* in 1912, Cather focused on book and drama reviews and observations gleaned from the world of art. While writing about art and artists, she was also formulating her artistic theories, and the sheer bulk and enormous scope of her material inevitably shaped her views.

Literary historians and social constructionists agree that the latter part of the nineteenth century was a fortuitous moment in gay history. Interest in homosexuality and ways of expressing homosexual sentiments coincided with changing attitudes toward art and sex, and challenges of gender assumptions altered literary representations of men and women. Robert K. Martin suggests that by the 1880s "homosexuality seems to have emerged sufficiently so that it has a public profile (certain authors, certain poems, certain subjects), while in the 1840s it was indistinguishable from other forms of male friendship" ("Knights-Errant" 181). Likewise, Linda Dowling argues that "Although it would be abruptly brought to an end as a cultural era, in 1895 by the catastrophe of Wilde's trial and imprisonment, the 1890s represented a cultural space within which may be glimpsed the major trends of a subsequent twentieth-century struggle for homosexual tolerance and civil rights, a fully developed language of moral legitimacy, of physical wholesomeness, of the psychic richness, beauty, and creativity of male love" (27). Cather's "kingdom of art" lay within this context, a cultural flux that witnessed the emergence of a diverse discourse on homosexuality, ranging from medical and legal hostility to the idealization of belles lettres. Bernice Slote condenses Cather's stance at this time to a resolutely primitivistic position: "The world was haunted by a divinity, there were forces on the earth and in heaven greater and more mysterious than man could interpret. She chose action and power; emotion, sympathy, and life. She rejected whatever was effete, over refined, or delicate. She rejected, too, whatever was hard and intellectually inhuman" ("First Principles" 33).

Cather's early decisions, however, are not always absolute; rather than definitive, her published commentaries are more often exploratory and reveal a young writer gradually discovering new ideas in a world of ideological change. Nowhere is this filtering process better illustrated than in Cather's response to Walt Whitman and Oscar Wilde, the two most prominent figures in the development of homosexual literature and modern gay identity. Part of Whitman's legacy is an explicitly homoerotic "love of comrades," while part of Wilde's is an implicitly homosexual "love that dared not speak its name." For Cather, Whitman is a "joyous elephant" and "optimistic vagabond," his poetry "sometimes sublime, sometimes ridiculous" (KA 351–53). Similarly, Wilde is "a harlequin," and his imprisonment, she hoped, marked the end of the aesthetic movement, "the most fatal and dangerous school of art that has ever voiced itself in the English tongue" (389). Although Cather's criticism ridiculed and disparaged both men, growing irate and even hostile, it also showed sympathy and admiration. Cather was both fascinated and repelled by the men and their work, and one needs merely to trace their influence in her writing to sense this paradoxical hold upon her imagination and, consequently, the impact of the homosexual challenge they embodied.[1]

By revealing an indirect response to an emerging gay sensibility, Cather's journalism uncovers an important link in her creative process. O'Brien notices a similarity in Cather's description of Alphonse Daudet's novel *Sapho* and the phrasing of her essay "The Novel Démeublé," showing the unorthodox literature that helped shape Cather's aesthetics (EV 136), and Slote traces the "glittering and allusive texture" encoding Cather's early fiction to her experience as a journalist ("First Principles" 92). Such allusive density underscores the intertextuality I am proposing, but it also poses for readers a peculiar dilemma not unlike Cather's own. The nineteenth-century classics Cather admired were written by men, and as O'Brien asks, "How could a woman be a legitimate heir of this exalted tradition?" (EV 81). We might also ask how a female can inherit a male homosexual legacy. If the sense of a shared sexuality defines that tradition, Cather remains permanently outside its borders. But by suffusing a homosexual sensibility into her aesthetics, Cather subverts the male tradition handed down to her while simultaneously making the homosexual tradition her own.[2]

Classical, Medieval, and Renaissance

It is perhaps appropriate that Cather borrowed from the homosexual tradition, for in a befitting literary irony, the work that many regard as the first novel, Petronius's *Satyricon*, is considered a gay text—one detailing "the adventures of a pair of dissolute youths as they wander through the decaying scenery of the Roman Empire" (Young, "The Flower" 149). But Cather's affiliation with homosexual literary traditions extends beyond imperial Rome and reaches back as far as ancient Greece.

Cather's familiarity with the classics is abundantly documented. As a young girl she studied Latin and Greek; at the University of Nebraska, she took a number of elective courses, including Greek lyric poetry, in the classics department; and after graduation she taught high school Latin in Pittsburgh (Slote, introduction x–xi). Her well-known essay honoring Sappho appeared in the *Nebraska State Journal* in 1895: "If of all the lost richness we could have one master restored to us, one of all the philosophers and poets, the choice of the world would be for the lost nine books of Sappho. Those broken fragments have burned themselves into the consciousness of the world like fire. All great poets have wondered at them, all inferior poets have imitated them. Twenty centuries have not cooled the passion in them. Sappho wrote only of one theme, sang it, laughed it, sighed it, wept it, sobbed it" (ĸA 349). Cather's review also contains a less-often-remembered reference to Anacreon, the Greek poet she read as a young girl and wrote variations upon as a university student. This knowledge of Greek lyric poetry is noteworthy, for as Vern Bullough suggests, "In lyric poetry, the most direct expression we have of the personal state of mind and feeling of the ancient Greeks, homosexual love occupied a major place. Unfortunately, only small fragments of the lyric poets have survived" (110). Cather's early reading of these fragments foretells her emotional reaction that Sappho's lyre, "like Anacreon's, responded only to a song of love" (ĸA 349). And in Anacreon's odes that solitary theme found expression in love between men.

Part of Cather's classicism is a gay heritage encompassing a rich tradition of literary, intellectual, and social history. John Addington Symonds, the nineteenth-century Renaissance scholar and early advocate of homosexual rights, overviews this cultural phenomenon: "For the student of sexual inversion, ancient Greece offers a wide field for observation and reflection. Its importance has hitherto been underrated by medical and legal writers on the subject, who do not seem to be aware that here alone in history have we the example of a great and highly-developed race not only tolerating homosexual passions, but deeming them of spiritual value, and attempting to utilize them for the benefit of society" (9). While repeated praise of male pairs occurs in Greek literature and history, Achilles and Patroclus emerge as antiquity's most famous friends. Regarded "as one of the highest products of their emotional life" (Symonds 12), their friendship sanctioned among the Greeks a form of masculine love and established the archetype for the Homeric ideal. The myth of Achilles and Patroclus, however, creates interpretative problems similar to those suggested by Cather's male pairs. Homer idealizes male love, but his depiction of it is often ambiguous. While Symonds reasons that the poet "knew nothing of paiderastia" (13), or Greek love in its physical sense, modern readers like Peter Green reinterpret the poet's reticence: "Though this relationship is not delineated in crudely sexual terms, the mythic tradition was well aware of its motivation, and Homer himself abundantly and repeatedly stresses the intensity and closeness of the two heroes' feeling for one another: if not homosexual in presentation, it is most certainly homoerotic" (24). Acknowledgment of Homer's "cultivated sensitivity" (Green 25) points to a similar refinement in Cather. Her presentation of male love relies on evocation rather than explicit description, the suggestiveness of "the thing not named" rather than specific detail.

Plato's contribution to a classical sensibility further informs Cather's aesthetics. Plato aligns male love with ideas of beauty, virtue, and spiritual development, and this inherent morality delineates the moral view Cather presents in her fiction. In his dialogues

Plato also makes a philosophical virtue of sexual restraint that Cather transmutes into an artistic virtue as well.

From this background in Greek literature, Cather found patterns of same-sex friendships matching her emotional life and literary tastes. Sappho and Homer offered models of same-sex love, ennobled by heroic action and social respect. Plato provided a philosophy that elevated male love above derision and contempt. Imaginatively excited by the literature of the ancient world, Cather turned these works into literary models and recreated in her fiction both their noble spirit and "erotic psychology" (Crompton 134).

Cather also discovered analogues for male friendship in Latin literature. As John Boswell points out, "Probably the most famous pair of lovers in the Roman world were Hadrian and Antinous" (CSTH 84). Although Hadrian, the peaceful Roman emperor, and Antinous, the Greek youth he loved and deified, had become conventional poetic symbols by the end of the nineteenth century, the emotional resonance of their relationship echoes throughout history.[3] Thus when Cather alludes, as she frequently does in *April Twilights* (1903), to the brooding beauty, mortal misery, and early death of Antinous, she brings to her poetry the enduring aura of a homosexual myth that, as Mary Ruth Ryder comments, furnishes a classical model for the protagonists of her later fiction (54).

While the classical tradition of male friendship stirred Cather's imagination, so too did the literary form it frequently took. The pastoral tradition, so often noticed in Cather's fiction, provides insights into a homosexual sensibility, invoking as it does "a tradition of poetry in which the love of men played a major and honorable part" (Martin, HT 58). In fact, the term *Arcadian*, like *Hellenic*, is often used euphemistically to arouse such feelings, derived from the *Idylls* of Theocritus as well as Corydon's love for Alexis in Virgil's second eclogue. The association of a Hellenistic eros within an Arcadian setting appears to such an extent in Western literature that Rictor Norton suggests that "If any particular genre can be called a homosexual genre, the evidence would point most convincingly to the pastoral tradition" (HLT 132). Jacob Stockinger goes further and argues for "homotextual space" in gay literature, a narrative strategy underscoring a proclivity among gay writers for certain genres (143). In this sense the "homotextuality" of the pastoral tradition both perpetuates the classical prototype and demonstrates its narrative flexibility. Such explorations of form provocatively color Cather's adaptation of classical literature: although she successfully transforms the pastoral tradition into texts of female heroism, her simultaneous celebration of all-male friendship continues to evoke its Greek ideal.

Just as the classical heritage has persisted in Western thought, so too has its gay traditions: "Wherever Ovid was enjoyed, Vergil quoted, Plato read, there gay passions and sentiments were known and studied and often respected" (Boswell, CSTH 210). While the Renaissance is traditionally recognized as the age of greatest classical revival, the period of the Middle Ages has been increasingly re-envisioned, and wider perceptions of its cultural diversity enhance the medieval aura Cather often evokes in her fiction. Of the Middle Ages in general, R. W. Southern believes that "the period from about 1100 to about 1320 to have been one of the great ages of humanism in the history of Europe: perhaps the greatest of all" (31). In *Christianity, Social Tolerance, and Homosexuality* John Boswell tests the strength of this humanism while simultaneously challenging historical assumptions: "Indeed the Middle Ages are often imagined to have been a time of almost universal intolerance of nonconformity, and the adjective 'medieval' is not infrequently used as a synonym for 'narrow-minded,' 'oppressive,' or 'intolerant' in the context of behavior or attitudes. It is not, however, accurate or useful to picture medieval Europe and its institutions as singularly and characteristically intolerant" (3). Traditions of homosexual literature support Boswell's claim for a level of tolerance during the Middle Ages, and while there exists evidence of homosexual poetry located specifically in religious communities, traces of a secular tradition further promulgate the concept of medieval humanism.[4]

Certainly the classical revival reached its high point during the Renaissance, and with it came a literary resurgence of Greek love traditions. Explanations for this revival can be traced to acquisition of new attitudes toward friendship by Englishmen during their visits to Italy in the sixteenth century as well as the availability of classical and early Renaissance texts dealing with friendship such as Cicero's *De amicitia*, Plato's *Symposium*, Marsilio Ficino's *Commentary on Plato's Symposium on Love*, and Baldassare Castiglione's *Book of the Courtier* (Lell 101–02). Shakespeare's texts provide the most resilient touchstone for a study of homosexuality in the Renaissance and offer a valuable analogue for Cather's representations. According to Graham Jackson, "The ambivalence in many of Shakespeare's characters perhaps qualifies him as one of the first playwrights to show a marked homosexual sensibility" (164). As her essay on *Hamlet* indicates, Cather responded to Shakespeare's wide human sympathy, especially as he portrays the friendship between Hamlet and Horatio—for her, not only the most beautiful thing in the play but the most beautiful friendship in all of Shakespeare. "Shakespeare," Cather writes, "was master of [the] few elementary emotions which are the keystone of life" (KA 436). Homosexual interpretations of Shakespeare's plays and sonnets extend these elementary emotions to include expressions of sexual diversity during the sixteenth century. Likewise, gay readings of Christopher Marlowe provide a vigorous dialectic in which to consider the cultural and literary manifestations of homosexuality during the Renaissance and their impact upon rival playwrights.[5]

American

Just as homosexuality suffuses the classical legacy, so too does it figure in the American literature handed down to Cather. Unfortunately, recognition of Cather as part of the "great tradition of American writing" (Edward and Lillian Bloom 237) overlooks this heritage. Yet while Cather's inheritance from nineteenth-century American literature affiliates her with a national literary tradition, her connection with its homosexual aspects places her as a direct descendant in the line of gay American literature.

According to Roger Austen, the nineteenth-century American

public was often inclined to interpret homoeroticism in its literature as synonymous with friendship (PG 7), a blurred outlook fuel-
ing Leslie Fiedler's argument that an "innocent homosexuality" (xi)
is the unconscious theme of the American novel. Recent critics,
however, reject Fiedler's approach and replace the term *homosexual*
with the seemingly more accurate *homosocial*. Accordingly, social—
not sexual—relations between men are now seen as unifying American literature from Cooper's *Leatherstocking Tales* through Herman
Melville's novels of men at sea and Henry James's bachelor stories.
As James Levin explains, homosexual themes in this literature are
either "hidden from all but the most diligent literary sleuth" or
"must be developed from a complex web of interpretations of symbolic passages or, otherwise, by a treatment of all male companion-
ships as if they were homoerotic" (10).

Other critics respond differently to the ambivalent archetypes of
American literature. Austen recognizes Melville as the "godfather
of homosexual fiction in this country" (PG 17), and Eve Kosofsky
Sedgwick has selected *Billy Budd* as one of the texts that inaugurated modern gay literary discourse (EC 49). Perhaps the work of
Robert K. Martin has made the most lucid case for reading certain
nineteenth-century texts as products of America's gay literary nas-
cence. Unlike Fiedler, Martin identifies a homophilic rather than a
homophobic strain in American literature and selects Whitman
and Melville to foster a canon of gay American literature.

In his groundbreaking work, *The Homosexual Tradition in American Poetry*, Martin announces that "The study of homosexuality in
American poetry begins with Walt Whitman" (xvi). Supporting
this claim, Austen observes that "By 1900 Whitman was recognized by the cognoscenti as *the* gay American poet" (PG 6), and
Sedgwick adds that "Whitman—visiting Whitman, liking Whitman, giving gifts of 'Whitman'—was of course a Victorian homosexual shibboleth, and much more that that, a step in the consciousness and self-formation of many members of that new
Victorian class, the bourgeois homosexual" (BM 28). And by subtly
constructing a homosexual hierarchy in *American Renaissance*, F. O.

Matthiessen seems to answer the call that Whitman makes in "A Backward Glance o'er Travel'd Roads" for "a shifted attitude from superior men and women towards the thought and fact of sexuality, as an element in character, personality, the emotions, and a theme in literature" (LG 572).[6] Read in this context, Cather's review of *Leaves of Grass* in 1896 signifies more than its brevity implies. While Woodress traces the line of American literature from "Emerson to Whitman to Willa Cather" (LA 159), Whitman's singular position in the homosexual literary tradition bestows to Cather a significantly broader inheritance.

Whitman's poetry furthers the interpretative debate over male love and friendship, and the ways *Leaves of Grass* has been read reflect the range of this argument. Martin judiciously draws its theoretical boundaries:

> Probably no body of poems, except perhaps Shakespeare's sonnets, has aroused so much controversy as Whitman's "Calamus." The reason for this is clear: readers' reactions to "Calamus" have depended on their responses not merely to the poetry but even more to the man they have found there. Since most readers have been heterosexual and have shared the prevailing American attitude that homosexuality represents not sexual choice but moral turpitude, they have found it impossible to react to these poems apart from their moral, or moralistic, responses to homosexuality. So, as with criticism of the sonnets, there have been two principal, apparently opposed, approaches. One has recognized that the poems are indeed depictions and even celebrations of love between men, and has condemned them for immorality and abnormality. The other has attempted to reconcile a distaste of homosexuality with a high regard for Whitman's poetry or his political and religious ideas; this approach has denied that the poems depict homosexuality, insisting that they be read metaphorically or as depictions of an ideal, i.e., asexual, friendship. Although these two approaches result in vastly different attitudes toward Whitman, their source is in a similar moral position and a shared assumption that homosexual content in a work of art invalidates the work. (HT 47–48)

Maintaining the analogy between the "Calamus" poems and Shakespeare's sonnets, Sedgwick argues that "both texts have figured importantly in the formation of a specifically homosexual (not just homosocial) male intertextuality" and observes that, like the sonnets, "Calamus" has forced critics working outside the homosexual tradition "to confront its issues, speak its name, and at least formulate their working assumptions on the subject" (BM 28). Because Cather writes within a Whitman tradition, this kinship invites opinions on the nature of her indebtedness to that line of descent. For besides providing a poetic model for the use of native materials, Whitman plays an iconic role as innovator of America's homosexual literary tradition.

While some readers interpret sexuality in *Leaves of Grass* literally, the tradition in Whitman studies has long upheld an allegorical model for reading his poetry. Ronald A. Sharp is perhaps representative of this approach when he argues against any single-minded reading of *Leaves of Grass* that would deny the inherent fluidity between sex and friendship: "But must we rescue the poems' homosexual dimensions by denying—or at least ignoring—their concern with friendship? Certainly these poems record experiences and yearnings, ecstasies and anxieties that we see less accurately if we insist on desexualizing them. But there is something narrow and profoundly unlike Whitman about regarding the theme of friendship only as a metaphor for sexuality, even if it does, at one level, serve that function" (75).

Where do such interpretations as these lead? Is one more promising than the other, and does either one alone adequately explicate the poetry? Asking these questions with regard to Whitman, in turn, anticipates our asking them concerning Cather, for the interpretative dilemma he poses is similar to hers, and consequently, potential answers about his poetry may inform our response toward her fiction.

Walt Whitman is perhaps America's most capacious poet and most expansive literary influence. He makes that idea clear when in *Song of Myself* he exclaims, "I am large, I contain multitudes" (LG

88), and ongoing criticism of his poetry is indebted to his inclusive vision. Both the content and the form of *Leaves of Grass* share this boast as Whitman's characteristic tallying, and successive editions display a democratic and democratizing vision, "all of which he finds implicit in friendship" (Sharp 76). But must friendship and homosexuality be mutually exclusive categories in Whitman? Can friendship be both the perfect metaphor of his egalitarian vision *and* a euphemism encoding male love such as "Hellenic" and "Arcadian"? And, if so, what is Whitman saying about the place of homosexuality in American life and in its national literature?

Martin explores these questions by interpreting the "Calamus" poems as texts "coincid[ing] with and defin[ing] a radical change in historical consciousness: the self-conscious awareness of homosexuality as an identity" (HT 51–52).[7] But politicizing Whitman's poems surpasses self-definition alone and engenders new cultural standards. Whitman's capacious boast invokes a multitude of personae from "a rough" to "the tenderest lover," and this range of male identities poses a direct challenge to nineteenth-century gender expectations. On one hand, the "Calamus" works are love poems, not addressing social issues; on the other, they are complex texts of social and sexual identity often at variance with cultural norms. "To call oneself 'the tenderest lover,'" as Martin points out, "is to accept one's femininity or, more accurately, to challenge all social prescriptions of behavior according to gender. . . . [A]nd it is precisely thus, as an opponent of dominant social values, as an exponent of the 'feminine' in culture, that Whitman asks to be remembered" (HT 69–70).

The consequences of this social defiance create a relatively new kind of art, exemplified by Whitman's poetry in the nineteenth century and Cather's fiction in the twentieth. Martin emphasizes the ideological affinity between the writing of women and gay men:

> It has traditionally been thought that "great" art must have political or social aims and that only "minor" art could concern itself with feelings. By renouncing the art of the world for the art of personal

experience, Whitman is making a choice similar to that made by many female artists. A woman can, of course, adopt the standards of "male" art. But many women have insisted on the validity of a "female" art, which explicitly rejects politics and war as the subjects suitable for art. . . . As long as art is popularly presumed to be an expression of the values of the dominant class (male heterosexuals), then the artist will be obliged to deal with those values in his or her work. . . . What begins to occur in the work of women and homosexuals is a questioning of those values, by the simple decision to abandon them. Whitman's "Calamus" poems are revolutionary, because no one (since Virgil at least) had written, "He loves him"; instead they had written, "He loves her" and "He kills him." (HT 81)

It is in a similar challenge that Cather strikingly resembles Whitman and reveals her indebtedness to the American homosexual literary tradition. Early in her career Cather endorsed masculine values to the extent of ridiculing and distrusting female writers. Her commentary on the demands of art clearly capitulates to an ideology of compulsive masculinity:

I have not much faith in women in fiction. They have a sort of sex consciousness that is abominable. They are so limited to one string and they lie so about that. They are so few, the ones who really did anything worth while; there were the great Georges, George Eliot and George Sand, and they were anything but women, and there was Miss Bronte who kept her sentimentality under control, and there was Jane Austen who certainly had more common sense than any of them and was in some respects the greatest of them all. Women are so horribly subjective and they have such scorn for the healthy commonplace. When a woman writes a story of adventure, a stout sea tale, a manly battle yarn, anything without wine, women and love, then I will begin to hope for something great from them, not before. (KA 409)

Certainly Cather's ambivalent response to Whitman played a part in her decision to abandon the "chesty manner" of the Kipling school (Cather, "Crane's *Wounds*" 68) and eventually separate creativity from masculinity.[8] Subverting male myths, either by making them female or by embellishing them with homosexual overtones, Cather poses her own challenge to gender restrictions and artistic demands. While Cather does not deal directly with social issues in her fiction, her challenge is implicit in her respect for friendship, and this esteem provides the basis for her social critique. Likewise, Whitman does not address social questions in "Calamus," but his vision in those poems and the love they celebrate provide the foundation for social change.[9] Similarly, when Cather reenvisions the masculine ideal by an encoding of homosexual paradigms, she too is making a radical break with the male-dominated, heterosexual literature before her, while at the same time extending the homosexual tradition inherited from Whitman.

To offer something new and unnamed, Whitman sought the freshness and vigor of a new word, a search providing an instructive corollary to Cather's own aesthetics. Whitman was interested in a word that would remove the negative connotations of *sodomy* or *invert* that were accessible to him from religious and scientific discourse.[10] While his poetry offers a range of terms to suggest his emotional truth—such as "camerado," "eleve," and "word unsaid"—the word *adhesiveness* most fully realizes Whitman's artistic aims: "His appropriation of the word 'adhesiveness' was an essential part of the process of validating love between men. As he used it, it lost its phrenological associations and took on new ones; it evoked the qualities Whitman admired—loyalty, fidelity, sharing, touching. It was to be the new word of a new religion" (Martin, HT 35).[11] For Whitman, suggestiveness is essential to creation, whether in his characteristic cataloguing or in his choice of a word to describe "manly love." Rather than a word to signify specific meaning, however, Cather's "thing not named" creates ongoing truth by evoking multiple possibilities.

Cather's exploration of male love and masculine desire becomes one of the Whitmanesque elements recurring throughout her fiction. However, another trend in American literature—the genteel, or academic, tradition, represented by writers like Charles Warren

Stoddard, Bayard Taylor, and Fitz-Greene Halleck, "the first poet of friendship in America" (Martin, HT 98)—offers an alternative to Whitman's "adhesiveness." As Cather is often placed in the genteel tradition, its presentation of male friendship, radically different from Whitman's, also shapes her aesthetics.[12] Although a homoerotic impulse played a significant part in the flourishing of this tradition, its literary manifestation is chiefly nonphysical. Among the values endorsed by the genteel writers are a respect for romantic friendship and male beauty and a corresponding view of women as either "Muse" or "mother" (Martin, HT 90). While lacking in phallic imagery and depictions of sexual acts, the genteel poets' most passionate experiences, as Martin observes, are "likely to be rendered as an idyllic afternoon on the grass, a deep look into a friend's eyes, or an understanding of brotherhood, rather vaguely defined" (HT 90).

Bayard Taylor's *Joseph and His Friend* (1870) is representative of the genteel tradition and stands today as a remarkable document in the literature of male friendship. Martin places Taylor at the center of a "homosexual literary circle" and the one among it who is most "concerned with homosexual definition" (HT 106). *Joseph and His Friend* is both an idealized depiction of male friendship and an early tract for gay rights. By combining emotionally charged language with pastoralized settings, Taylor conveys the politics and polemics of male love: "They took each other's hands. The day was fading, the landscape was silent, and only the twitter of nesting birds was heard in the boughs above them. Each gave way to the impulse of his manly love, rarer, alas! but as tender and true as the love of women, and they drew nearer and kissed each other. As they walked back and parted on the highway, each felt that life was not wholly unkind, and that happiness was not yet impossible" (217). Commenting upon the author's unusual candor and courage, Martin writes: "Within the framework of a thoroughly genteel novel, Taylor creates a world that seems astonishingly close to 'Calamus'" (HT 103). Here too is another correspondence between Cather and the homosexual tradition in American literature. Similarly heightened scenes of male love and friendship recur in Cather's narratives and place her fiction somewhere between the Whitman tradition of symbolic sexuality and the genteel tradition of decorum and restraint.

Affiliation with forgotten texts as well as affinities with sexual aspects of familiar literature opens new vistas into Cather's art. Her kinship with Whitman and the genteel writers inextricably connects her with the history of the homosexual literary tradition in nineteenth-century America and gives her a role in charting its future course. For Martin, the defeat of the genteel writers by the emerging cult of masculinity and Whitman's "self-defeat" by the "almost insuperable obstacles," "enormous crudity," and "magnificent tastelessness" of his poetry marked the failure of the challenge they posed to cultural norms: "But there has existed in America no literary tradition that has successfully combined the frank sexuality and direct confrontation of the social and political issues of sexuality, which are the contribution of Whitman, with a real strength and purity of language, no works that could become essential parts of the literary imagination. This has happened in other places— with Shakespeare's sonnets, for instance, or with Stefan George in Germany or Gide in France" (HT 92). Although lacking "frank sexuality," the ambiguity of Cather's sexual aesthetics nonetheless helped sustain the American homosexual literary tradition in the early decades of the twentieth century.

British

Connections with British texts further strengthen Cather's contributions to the development of modern gay literature. As it does in American fiction and poetry, "Homoeroticism suffuses nineteenth-century British literature" (Summers, *Gay Fictions* 20), and Cather's affiliation with Oscar Wilde, Walter Pater, and A. E. Housman informs readers of her indebtedness to Victorian writers and trends associated with homosexuality.

Reaction to Walt Whitman's outspokenness helped set the stage for the development of British homosexual literature in the second half of the nineteenth century, a response shaped in part by John Addington Symonds's ardent praise that "Yet no man in the modern world has expressed so strong a conviction that 'manly attachment,' 'athletic love,' the 'high towering love of comrades,' is a main factor in human life, a virtue upon which society will have to rest, and a passion equal in its permanence and intensity to sexual affection" (183). Whether through his admiring prose, his probing correspondence with the poet, or his own Whitmanesque verse, Symonds expounded a homoerotic interpretation of *Leaves of Grass* and sought to establish a link between Whitman and Hellenic values, especially a Neoplatonism that esteemed emotional intimacy between men. When he praises Whitman as "Greek," he anticipates Cather's own description of the poet's "primitive elemental force" (KA 352) that recognizes the naturalness of every human impulse.[13]

Another prominent English admirer of Whitman was Edward Carpenter, who, unlike Symonds, advocated a physical expression of homosexual love. Although Sedgwick observes that "overt male homosexual style in England and America in this century has had few ties to the Edward Carpenter tradition" (BM 217), tension in Cather's fiction seems at times to indirectly enact a Victorian drama between the real and the ideal, the expressive and the repressed, as exemplified by divergent responses to Whitman and later fictionalized in E. M. Forster's *Maurice* (1971). The protagonist's dilemma in that novel is not that of choosing between homosexuality or heterosexuality but, rather, of choosing between the homosexuality defined by Symonds and that defined by Carpenter. Selecting the spontaneous Alec over the inhibited Clive, Maurice eventually experiences spiritual growth through a relationship that includes sexual intimacy.

While Whitman may have begun modern gay literature in America and paved the way for its development elsewhere, "Modern gay fiction in England," as Claude J. Summers declares, "begins with Oscar Wilde" (*Gay Fictions* 29). In addition to the homosexual content of works like "The Portrait of Mr. W. H.," *The*

Picture of Dorian Gray, and *De Profundis*, Summers sees Wilde's role in gay history, like Whitman's, "as a symbolic figure who exemplified a way of being a homosexual at a pivotal moment in the emergence of gay consciousness" (29). And just as Cather voiced an ambivalent response to Whitman in her journalism, so too does she similarly respond to Wilde, whom she at first perceived as threatening the cultural and artistic virility she upheld at the time. Cather demanded of artists a strict, almost ascetic, discipline; she also ridiculed any effeminacy, preferring more "manly" artists like Kipling, and she found football more invigorating and wholesome than witty, drawing-room conversation. Likewise, action rather than conversation made a good play. The flamboyant Wilde shattered Cather's youthful expectations and seemed intentionally to mock her "kingdom of art."

As in her criticism of Whitman, Cather's ambivalence toward Wilde is felt throughout her critical statements and is suggested by the direction of her fiction. It is further evidenced by her seemingly contradictory stance during the 1890s, marked by disparagement of Wilde along with adulation of Paul Verlaine, leading Summers to suppose that "Cather's principal objection to Wilde is as much personal as it is literary" (*Gay Fictions* 65). But while Wilde was universally acknowledged, he was not universally praised. As Thomas E. Yingling suggests, part of the anxiety induced by the homosexual aura of the aesthetic movement was "the fear of cultural depletion, of the sapping of the empire's strength" (11–12). For Cather, Wilde's aestheticism saps artistic strength, and her "unremittingly hostile" (Summers, *Gay Fictions* 63) reviews register its harmful effects. Frowning on Wilde's dandyism and decadent posturing, Cather considers him dangerous and unhealthy.

Cather's commentary, like her fiction, is often difficult to decode; in fact, it is not immediately clear what she is referring to in her attacks on Wilde, whether his plays, his persona, or both. There is an odd cleverness about her criticism too, something curiously Wildean in her ambivalence. Two possibilities seem likely: she may have been condemning homosexuality by condemning

Wilde, or she may have been enlisting cultural attitudes about homosexuality to frame a response to Wilde's artistry. Given Cather's exploratory stance at the time and her habit of questioning gender assumptions, I would argue the latter. Turning social hostility toward homosexuality into a rhetorical means to criticize Wilde's writing, Cather exploits the negative connotations of expressions like "deepest infamy," "darkest shame," and "sinned the sin" (KA 391–92) to discredit his art. Close reading reveals that, for Cather, Wilde threatened not ethics but aesthetics; thus she launched an attack based upon the morality of art, not the morality of the artist.

Cather's comments on Paul Verlaine and Algernon Swinburne reinforce this strategy by carefully distinguishing between respect for an artist and appreciation of his art. "The poet's chief concern is not with his life, but his work," Cather wrote in 1896. And if poets "stumble," continued Cather, "it is because they watch the stars" (KA 396–97). In language similar to her praise of Sappho, Cather describes Swinburne as "thoroughly a Greek, in his thought and treatment, as well as in his theme," yet she calls him a "mighty singer" and "the greatest living English poet indeed" following Tennyson's death and Wilde's imprisonment (KA 349–50). Awed by Verlaine's genius, Cather is humbled and forgiving and writes that although he was "the grossest of sensualists"—"a practicer of every excess known to man" and "imprisoned again and again for unmentionable and almost unheard of crimes"—nonetheless he was "the most exalted of the devotional mystics" and "wrote some of the most beautiful and devout religious poetry in any tongue" (KA 394).

Toward Wilde, Cather is less charitable. While his extravagant enactment of the suffering artist and his playing out the role of the aesthete may have heightened her disdain for his "epigrammatics" (KA 135), the waste of his genius rather than his sexual choice makes him infamous, and a lack of sincerity is his greatest sin; these faults make his books, like Ouida's, "one rank morass of misguided genius and wasted power . . . sinful, not for what they do, but for what they do not do" (KA 409). Cather further attacks Wilde's "absurd mannerisms" (KA 135) in her review of an adaptation of *The Green Carnation* (1894), Robert Hichens's parody of Wilde and his circle. The English, Cather feels, lack epigrammatic talent, and regarding an Englishman's trying to be French, Cather warns that "The affectation poisons his style, his vigor and his whole personality. He loses not only his art but his manhood" (KA 136). For Cather, Wilde's most unforgivable crimes are not those he commits against society but against literature and himself.

Given the extremity of Cather's comments, it is perhaps surprising to look for traces of Wilde in her fiction and even more surprising to find them. Yet Cather's public stance toward Wilde significantly differs from her artistic assimilation. At times Cather's journalism echoes the condemning language of the Crown prosecutor at Wilde's trial. Her fiction, however, evokes Wilde's eloquent self-defense, his allusive praise of male love that moved the court to applause if not acquittal. Beneath Wilde's decorative surface other links exist between his and Cather's art, such as the indirection of *The Picture of Dorian Gray*, subjectivity in "The Portrait of Mr. W. H.," and the value of sympathy in *De Profundis*. Wilde's specific contributions to gay literature also anticipate Cather's own, including, as Summers indicates, "The preoccupation with self-realization, the opposition of the individual and society, the yearning for an escape from moralistic strictures, the exploring of connections between Eros and art, the search for a gay golden age and for the recovery of the past (often imagined as Arcadian or Hellenistic), and the depiction of divided selves" (*Gay Fictions* 60). But just as Wilde overshadowed the homosexual tradition in the late nineteenth century, so too did Cather's opinion of him overshadow her admiration for other writers associated with the aesthetic movement. Likewise the critical focus on Cather's disparagement of Wilde diverts attention from her affinities with British writers toward whom she was more sympathetic. While Cather frowned upon Wilde's artistic temperament, she did not totally dismiss aestheticism, for, like Wilde, she was heir to a homosexual aesthetic tradition, and her kinship with its theorists reveals close literary ties.

Cather's enthusiasm for Walter Pater—the "prophet of mysteries" (Arthur C. Benson 48) whom she had studied "with some intensity" (Slote, "First Principles" 36)—mitigates her disparagement of Wilde and underscores connections between a British homosexual sensibility and her own aesthetics. Interestingly it is Walter Pater to whom Cather refers in defining the goals of literary art: "Pater said that every truly great drama must, in the end, linger in the reader's mind as a sort of ballad. Probably the same thing might be said of every great story. It must leave in the mind of the sensitive reader an intangible residuum of pleasure; a cadence, a quality of voice that is exclusively the writer's own, individual, unique" ("The Best Stories" 49–50). Crucial to the quality of Pater's voice is an eroticized discourse, more specifically "a cultural ideal expressive of desire between men" (Dellamora 58). By opening the subject of sexual attraction and relations between men, Pater presented a challenge to the sexual norms of Victorian culture. The eroticized aesthetics of *The Renaissance*, for example, address sexual aspects of culture and celebrate male friendship in antiquity; in particular, Pater's chapter on Johann Winckelmann articulates a bond between homoeroticism and art "in which homosexual emotions were the paradigm of spiritual love" (Perrie 170). By conflating homosexuality and Christianity, *Marius the Epicurean* further extends Pater's liberality of thought and feeling.

Cather's aesthetics also have striking affinities with the Oxford Movement of Victorian poetry. As Wilde and his circle linked homosexuality and aestheticism, this movement's combination of homosexuality and religion affected both the spiritual and the sexual climate of Victorian literature. Ian Young describes its fusion of religion and sexuality: "In many writers, and especially in many of the Victorian writers, the religious impulse and the homosexual impulse were deeply meshed. The spiritual struggles of such men as Newman, Hopkins, Faber and Dolben, their idealistic striving and yearning for beauty and love, remained enmeshed in Christian injunctions, restrained by social convention, and channeled into acceptably orthodox (and celibate) pursuits" ("The Flower" 180). Whatever its motive in her personal life, Cather's artistic attraction to Catholicism in her fiction has a curious parallel with the Victorian homosexual literary tradition and its attraction to the rituals of chivalry and the church.

This sexual aesthetic awareness creates a homosocial/homosexual continuum in late Victorian literature similar to that in nineteenth-century America. While Brian Reade argues that Hopkins makes perhaps the most dramatic case for the links "between homosexual emotional crises and religious emotional crises" (12), Walter Perrie adds that the subdued "homoerotic components" (172) of Tennyson's "In Memoriam" significantly contributed to its vast popularity in the nineteenth century. Perhaps the Victorian poet most closely related to Cather's aesthetics, however, is A. E. Housman, whose *A Shropshire Lad* (1896) Cather describes as unmistakably genuine and true, "the like of which we have scarcely had in the last hundred years" (WCIE 27). Reade contemplates the erotic impact of Housman's poems: "*A Shropshire Lad* is like a beautiful ruin built over an invisible framework, and Housman obscured the framework so well that until recently not many readers of the poems seemed to guess that it was *l'amour de l'impossible* which haunted many of them" (48–49).

Cather was among the first to respond to Housman and to recognize in *A Shropshire Lad* "the hallmark of true poetry" (W&P 707). O'Brien suggests that Cather's enthusiasm combined "the excitement of discovery and the sureness of mutual understanding," pointing out that she was particularly drawn to Housman's themes of "exile, loneliness, and loss" that corresponded to her own loneliness in Pittsburgh in the late 1890s (EV 250). But Cather also may have responded to the emotional penumbra of Housman's verse, an inexplicable mood at the heart of his poetry. Reade locates this source of *A Shropshire Lad* in the oppressive sexual climate following Wilde's trial and defines Housman's particular depression as "the sadness of one who was doomed to live with unsuitable emotions in a community where these were tacitly recognized but officially condemned" (48).

The harshness of Cather's attacks on Wilde has its opposite in her admiration of Housman. That Cather was an admitted "bond slave" (Woodress, LL 158) to Housman draws attention to similarities in their work. While repeated allusions to Housman in *April Twilights* reveal her youthful excitement over the poet, his continued influence upon her fiction indicates a deeper, longer-lasting affinity. Homosexuality seems a likely touchstone to this kinship, contributing not only to the mystery of their art but to the mastery of their style as well, shaping alike the "unfinished" poetry of Housman and Cather's "unfurnished" novels.[14]

The late Victorian climate was one in which masculine ideals were being questioned, and homosexuals and gay literature were providing part of that gender challenge. As a young student and journalist, Cather was firmly defiant of—yet at the same time fascinated by—cultural change. While her statements about aestheticism seem harsh and unequivocal, they are made mostly in the context of Oscar Wilde, and for Cather it is his limitations that limit the aesthetic movement. By evoking homosexuality to reenvision masculinity, Cather echoes the eroticized discourse of Walter Pater and the Oxford poets, and in their conciliation of spiritual and erotic feelings, readers discover provocative analogues for the blending of romantic and religious overtones in her male friendships.

Ironically, Oscar Wilde also contributed to Cather's renunciation of the robust masculine aesthetic, and her ambivalence toward him draws attention to this indirect influence. "To note an artist's limitations is but to define his genius" ("The Best Stories" 54), Cather once stated, and in some ways this outlook clarifies her mixed feelings about Wilde and informs readers of the similarities rather than the differences between the two of them. One of Wilde's biographers writes that "We inherit his struggle to achieve supreme fictions in art, to associate art with social change, to bring together individual and social impulse, to save what is eccentric and singular from being sanitized and standardized, to replace a morality of severity by one of sympathy" (Ellmann 589). Greater experience with the world and her own maturing artistry gradually widened Cather's perspective to include much of this inheritance, and throughout her fiction she implicitly continues the challenges made by Wilde and her Victorian predecessors.

French

Cather's preference for Paul Verlaine over Oscar Wilde reflects in part her cultural fascination with all things French. As a university student, Cather exuberantly upheld the creative energy of France: "Stopping to think of it, most things come from France, chefs and salads, gowns and bonnets, dolls and music boxes, plays and players, scientists and inventions, sculptors and painters, novelists and poets. It is a very little country, this France, and yet if it were to take a landslide in the channel some day there would not be much creative power of any sort left in the world. Some psychologist said that all Frenchmen are more or less insane, but fortunately it is an insanity that so often takes the form of genius" (W&P 223). Cather continues this spirited devotion in her reviews of French literature, and in writing about her favorite authors, she transforms France into a cultural ideal.[15] French domesticity has generally been seen as a primary reason for this dedication, and many of the values Cather's fiction endorses have their model in the idealized French home and family. Yet French culture offered Cather other, less conventional fascinations, and French literature, in particular, drew her into a fictional world of unorthodox sexuality. Significantly, homosexual traditions are as much a part of the French culture Cather so enthusiastically embraced as are cooking, gardening, and housekeeping.

Critics and biographers provocatively dwell on Cather's glorification of France. Slote views it as a "positive image set against much that she found negative in America" ("First Principles" 61), an attitude derived in part from French Romanticism. O'Brien elaborates upon this literary influence: "French literature, particularly that of the southern regions of France, was Cather's passion during her college years and throughout her life. For her a warm, sensuous land bathed in light, Provence was linked in her imagination with the southern Mediterranean world—North Africa, Italy, Greece, Turkey, and Persia" ("'The Thing Not Named'" 588). "The French," Cather wrote, "are full of oriental feeling," and in France "The great passions never become wholly conventionalized" (KA 138). The word "oriental" colors Cather's commentaries and evokes her feeling for the exotic and "savage" (KA 138) undercurrents she found in French fiction.[16] Of this literary preference, O'Brien concludes that "France to Cather was the symbolic location of the Other, the sign for everything repressed or feared in commercial, puritanical northern climes: it was the decadent, liberated realm of the senses" ("'The Thing Not Named'" 589).

In sexual matters, French literature vastly differed from that of Britain and of America, and Cather's ability to read French admitted her into an uninhibited world. A comparatively tolerant legal system contributed to France's literary freedom. The Labouchère Amendment (1885) in England, under which Oscar Wilde was tried, criminalized homosexuality; in France the Napoleonic Code (1810) had abolished such a statute liability. While legal sanction alone does not remove social condemnation of sexual nonconformity, it does provide a larger scope to personal and artistic freedom. In addition to legal tolerance, France's cultural history also conditioned its response to diversity. As Boswell points out, traditional French love poetry had already established a cultural tolerance for sexual variance, and by the Middle Ages, expressions of homosexual love were unusually refined in France.[17]

An example of the sexual indulgences popular in the French novels Cather admired was a sensationalized focus on lesbianism. The presence of lesbianism in this literature presents an interesting parallel to Cather's own depiction of male friendship. Nineteenth-century French literary aesthetes expressed a hostility to middle-class morality and frequently used sexual nonconformity to voice their cry of "épater le bourgeoise." Among the most influential literary texts depicting unorthodox sexuality were Théophile Gautier's *Mademoiselle de Maupin* (1835), "the bible of aesthetic-decadent literature, and whose title character became a prototype of the lesbian in literature for decades afterward" (Faderman 264), Alphonse Daudet's *Sapho* (1884), a copy of which Cather "owned and valued" as early as 1891 (Slote, "First Principles" 38), and Gustave Flaubert's luridly sensual *Salammbô* (1862), which Cather admitted to liking the best of all his novels ("A Chance Meeting" 22).

What can one speculate about the influence of these novels upon Cather's fiction? While Cather did not seek to shock her readers overtly, neither was she timid in her writing. As she had made the British and American literary heritage her own, so too did she appropriate the French tradition. What is most striking in Cather's adaptation is that her handling of male homosexuality is significantly less ambivalent than is the treatment of lesbianism in French fiction. Neither cautionary nor sensational, Cather idealizes male friendship and links it to traditions of cultural and literary respect; rather than creating "moral monsters" (Faderman 272), Cather affirms same-sex relationships and, in doing so, carefully distinguishes her fiction from the popular French novels she enjoyed.

Neither the "decadent" tradition nor the realism of Honoré de Balzac, who included a homosexual relationship in his vast panorama of human experience, provided Cather with a model for her treatment of homosexuality; however, she found a precedent elsewhere in French literature. The death of Paul Verlaine in 1896 gave her an opportunity to eulogize the poet in her newspaper column and at the same time to contemplate the impact the French Symbolists made upon her imagination, and this commentary brings us very close to Cather's connection with the French homosexual literary tradition. Her thoughts about Verlaine offer a striking contrast to those about Wilde. Although cultural historians, such as Max Nordau in his widely read *Degeneration* (1895), considered them to be equally dangerous figures, Cather vindicated Verlaine while she condemned Wilde.[18]

Although it is tempting to see Cather's cultural bias toward

France as one explanation for her literary choices, more substantial reasons lie in her response to Verlaine's artistry and his experiments with poetry. While Cather's "art of suggestion" (David Stouck, "Impressionist Novel" 52) derives from the Symbolists and the Impressionists of the late nineteenth century, her artistic success can be attributed in part to the suggestion of homosexuality in their poetry. Perrie explains: "For English writers the chief gain from symbolism was not, at least until Eliot and Pound, a technical one, though the innovations by Verlaine and others in the use of language as an associative and connotative instrument for the expression of feelings were inseparable from their concern with subjectivity, but was, rather, a new willingness to explore areas of feeling previously prohibited to serious literature. By the 1870s homosexual feelings and relationships had become something of an established feature of French literature" (172).

Anticipating Eliot's and Pound's stylistic innovations by a decade or more, Cather gained from French poetry a recognition of both technical and thematic subtlety. Verlaine achieved in his poetry what Cather sought in her fiction, the evocation of "the thing not named," and she praises this skill in her reviews: "His verses are like music, they are made up of harmony and feeling, they are as indefinite and barren of facts as a nocturne. They tell only of a mood" (KA 395). Such praise resembles her sentiments on the discovery of A. E. Housman, and as she did with the English poet, Cather felt toward Verlaine an instinctive understanding and artistic kinship. It would be unlikely that she failed to see the homosexual resonance in his "feverish, overstrained, unnatural" poetry (Cather, W&P 648) and not recognize in it an important source of its haunting beauty.

But it was the French novelist Pierre Loti (pseudonym of Julien Viaud), distinguished naval officer and member of the prestigious French Academy, who most influenced Cather in this area. Among the forgotten or ignored influences upon Cather, Slote recalls Dumas, Daudet, and Pierre Loti ("First Principles" 32). While critics have explored Cather's affiliation with many of the nineteenth-century French romanticists, her connections with the once popular Loti have suffered the same neglect he and his work have suffered since his death in 1923.

At the end of the nineteenth century, Pierre Loti was perhaps France's most successful and prolific literary figure and was called the country's "greatest living writer" by Anatole France (Poggenbury 78). Although Loti wrote about such exotic places as North Africa, Japan, Tahiti, and Persia, he is often remembered, if he is remembered at all, for his Breton novels and the way in which he makes the rugged and lonely coast of Brittany appear "strangely different and fascinating" (Poggenbury 81).[19] While stylistic similarities exist between Loti's and Cather's rendering of subjective experience, whether of a rocky coastline or a wild prairie, to recognize Loti's deepest influence upon Cather is to recognize their similar treatment of male friendship and masculine desire.[20]

According to Slote, "By the spring of 1896 Willa Cather was familiar with most of the important French writers, but she had a special feeling for the style and themes of Pierre Loti" ("Critical Statements" 365). In Cather's review of *Le Roman d'un spahi* (*The Romance of a Spahi*), her sympathetic response to Loti's language indicates their stylistic affinities: "But ah, such description! All English description is odious. Careful, accurate, burdened with irrelevant detail, lifeless, leaving no picture in the reader's mind. But with the French it is a different matter. They write as they paint, to bring out an effect" (KA 367).

Other readers falling under Loti's evocative spell have commented upon his descriptive power more pointedly than Cather. In *The Intersexes*, for instance, Xavier Mayne includes Loti with about a dozen novelists—including Joris-Karl Huysmans (*À rebours* [*Against the Grain*], 1884) and Georges Eekhoud (*Escal-Vigor*, 1909)—who were dealing with gay themes in French. In 1907 E. M. Forster entered Loti's name in his diary as part of a growing list of names "directed in part toward discovering a homosexual literary tradition" (Martin, "Edward Carpenter" 37). But the most curious response to Loti comes from Henry James. In writing to

Owen Wister about *The Virginian*, James expresses his dissatisfaction with the ending of that novel. As Wister's hero seemingly betrays his friendship with Steve, in turn James feels Wister betrays the novel's distinctive mood by having the hero conventionally marry and suffer no remorse for the loss of his friend. James has strong "reserves" and calls the ending "mere *prosaic* justice, and rather grim at that" (LHJ 233). His suggestions for revision are unequivocal: "I thirst for his blood. I wouldn't have let him live and be happy; I should have made him perish in his flower and in some splendid noble way" (LHJ 233). To improve the ending, James directs Wister to Pierre Loti's *Pêcheur d'islande* (*An Iceland Fisherman*), a work Michael Moon describes as "perhaps the most pungently male homoerotic novel about a sailor before Jean Genet's *Querelle de Brest*" (260). The hero of Loti's novel similarly betrays the memory of his young friend and their idyllic life at sea by marrying soon after his friend's untimely death. His subsequent unhappiness and death have all the splendid nobility James envisioned as due recompense for Wister's hero.

Cather read *Pêcheur d'islande* in 1896 along with her friends the Seibels, whom she gifted with a charcoal portrait of the author that she had bought on her first trip to France ("First Principles" 60). In addition to *Pêcheur d'islande* (1886), "generally thought to be Loti's masterpiece" (Blanch 180), and *Le Roman d'un spahi* (1881), Cather was likely familiar with *Mon frère Yves* (*My Brother Yves*, 1883), "probably Loti's best-known book" (Blanch 128). Cather ends her review of *Le Roman d'un spahi* by recalling Loti's pull upon her imagination:

> I like to think of Pierre Loti, soldier, sailor and artist, sailing among his green seas and palm-fringed islands, through all the tropic nights and orient days. Anchoring at white ports and talking with wild men, now on the high seas and now the desert, which the ancients quaintly called a sea. We see too much of civilization, we know it all too well. It is always beating about our ears and muddling our brains. We sometimes need solitude and the desert, which

Balzac said was "God without mankind." Loti is a sort of knight-errant to bring it to us, who gives to [us] poor cold-bound, sense-dwarfed dwellers in the North the scent of sandalwood and the glitter of the southern stars. (KA 367)

If France is Cather's realm of romance, Loti's novels exemplify its imaginative appeal, evoking as they do melancholy, deep mystery, and homoerotic longings through an impressionistic prose style similar to the poetry of Verlaine and Housman. They provide Cather with a stylistic and thematic model for writing about men in love and the dilemma it poses both for characters attempting to name their feelings and for an author seeking to describe those feelings. Loti identifies this dilemma in the text itself, for what troubles his characters also seems to perplex their creator. Writing to one another when they are separated, the central characters of *Mon frère Yves* are at a loss as to how to begin their letters, uncertain of the appropriate salutation signifying their relationship. The word *brother* is selected, thus the title of the novel. However, Yves and Pierre's relationship seems more than brotherly—they live together, travel together, think only of one another when apart, and dream of each other at night.[21] Similar terminology can be found in American genteel fiction, such as Bayard Taylor's *Joseph and His Friend* and his short story "Twin Love" (1862). But here too the emotional power of Taylor's fiction surpasses friendship and familial love. As Martin points out, "The use of brothers appears to be a dodge, allowing for an expression of affection which would otherwise be unthinkable" (HT 101). Henry James similarly encodes erotic desire by offering himself as "a brother and a lover" (LHJ 226) in a consoling letter to his young friend Hendrik Andersen, toward whom James's biographers agree he was erotically attracted.[22]

While safe under the banner of "brother" and "friend," such relationships often push the boundaries of family and friendship into other areas of personal experience. Boswell writes that such ambiguous terms "evoke a wealth of associations secular and religious,

erotic and spiritual, paternal and lover-like. They are part of a tradition of erotic address between men which has no standard terms
of relation and has thus elicited the ambiguities of the Greek 'lover,
inspirer, hearer,' the Roman 'friend, brother, dear,' the monastic
'brother, son, friend, beloved brother,' and many other terms of
endearment for relationships without real parallel in heterosexual
contexts" (CSTH 193). In the absence of an adequate vocabulary to
express intimacy between men, familiar expressions thus assume
new meanings. Although Cather leaves her protagonists' relationships muted and unspecified, words like "friend," "brother," "son,"
and "father" echo the dynamics of ambiguous discourse and participate in the range of emotions Boswell describes.

Loti's influence upon Cather also exemplifies the power of imaginative experience. Haunted by Loti's vast sea spaces, Cather also
seems intrigued by the eroticization of those spaces. The recurrent
motif of the French sailor as an erotic symbol is particularly relevant here. A structural feature of Loti's novels is their all-male
tableaux, scenes of sailors on the open sea or in groups while on
shore leave. One example from *Mon frère Yves* illustrates Loti's pic-
torial style: "On the forecastle the men of the watch were singing
as they performed their morning ablutions. They looked like stat-
ues from the antique with their strong arms as they stood there
stripped, washing themselves in cold water, plunging their head
and shoulders into the deep tubs, covering their chests with a white
lather, and then separating into couples, with the greatest simplicity, to rub each other's backs" (208). Here the routine of bathing is
transformed into a ritual both religious and erotic. Throughout his
fiction Loti's tableaux depict such heightened moments of men together and convey powerful feelings through simplicity and restraint.

A well-known author once asserted that the sole purpose of the
French navy was to decorate the coast of France. Cather had a
firsthand opportunity to observe this decorative navy during her
European tour in 1902. Meeting a group of sailors in the streets of

La Seyne, she cheerfully sketches her impressions of that encounter:

> We stood for some moments in the middle of the street, surrounded by a crowd of voluble sailors, all chattering gaily in the most perplexing dialect. Edmund Dantes was everywhere, dressed exactly as we have all seen him on the stage, and as we have all imagined him in our childhood. Wide trousers of white duck, a navy-blue woolen jacket, the wide braided collar of his light blue cotton shirt reaching outside of his jacket and over his broad shoulders. He wore military moustaches, sometimes earrings, a white cotton tam-o'-shanter with a red tassel at the top, and a red sash about his waist. There were scores of him all about us. It occurred to us that some of our friends at home would be alarmed if they knew that we were standing in the middle of the sailors' quarter in a Mediterranean shipping town, quite alone, so late at night. But we saw about us only the most amiable brown faces, and when we asked where we could find a hotel, not one, but a score replied. They spoke faster and faster, and inserted dozens of perplexing expletives; they lined up and snatched off their caps and pointed out the direction for us, as the chorus of a light opera point and look expectantly when the strain that introduces the tenor sounds in the orchestra. A fine tableau they made, too, in the red lights from the café windows. (WCIE 147–48)

From the operetta-like stereotypes alluded to in this passage comes a glimpse of the "handsome sailor" so often seen in gay literature; like Edmund Dantes, Pierre Loti is also everywhere, in the scene before Cather and in the colorful scenario she offers a reader. Combining travel literature with impressionistic prose, Cather's description evokes Loti's male tableaux, his paean to sailors' youth, vitality, and untroubled intimacy, whether pressed together along a narrow street or splendidly poised aboard their ships. "The true pleasures of life," the narrator exclaims in *Mon frère Yves*, "are youth and health, with the simple joys of good animal spirits, and sailors' songs!" (165).

The French sailor is indicative of the overall exoticism of Loti's novels, an exoticism unexpectedly surfacing in Cather's fiction. At the church supper in *O Pioneers!*, for example, Marie's Bohemian costume and Emil's "conspicuous attire" (216)—his sombrero, silk sash, black velvet jacket, and turquoise shirt studs—provide striking details against the prairie landscape. Likewise, Captain Pondeven in *Shadows on the Rock*—his appearance, his parrot, even his dinner of Breton pancakes—recalls the exoticism of Loti's fiction. Cather's blending of the exotic with the erotic further recreates the mood of French literature, exemplified by variations of Loti's eroticized sailor in the handsome marine aboard the troopship in *One of Ours* and Godfrey St. Peter's seafaring fantasy in *The Professor's House*. Slote rightly feels that "To understand Willa Cather we will have to study the French Romantics" ("First Principles" 85); such study would reveal to us not only the influence of Dumas and Daudet upon Cather's fiction but also the lasting hold on her imagination of the "lost books" ("First Principles" 32) of Pierre Loti.

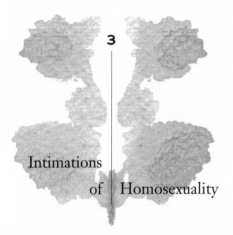

3

Intimations of Homosexuality

IN the introduction to *Willa Cather's Gift of Sympathy* Edward A. and Lillian D. Bloom describe their experience of reading Cather for the first time. While their recollection mirrors what has become an increasingly familiar reader response, it also provides a reference point for exploring the extent of Cather's sexual aesthetics:

> Like many others of Miss Cather's large audience, we began reading her novels with no motivation except to derive pleasure. Not only did we discover an abundance of enjoyment, but we soon found ourselves tempted to go back and reread—many times. Each reading became a fresh experience; familiar details became clearer, and springs hitherto unnoticed kept welling to the surface. By her own admission a practitioner of simplicity in art, Miss Cather affords the pleasures of uninvolved narration and yet embroiders and augments her stories with subtle layers of related meanings. Gradually, we felt that we were discovering a richness of esthetic and idea in her novels which no single or superficial reading could possibly reveal. (ix–x)

This temptation to reread is one result of Cather's "thing not named." But indirection opens other possibilities as well, for as soon as the "démeublé" process in Cather's fiction begins, intimations of homosexuality appear to assist in its unfurnishing. The more we uncover the ambiguity of Cather's art, the more its sexual implications unfold, and like the Blooms, we too discover an unexpected narrative richness.

Sexuality in Cather's texts has been for the most part underestimated by readers and critics alike. Loretta Wasserman points out that "A common observation about Willa Cather's fiction is that it fails to treat sex in any kind of adequate way" ("The Lovely Storm" 348). By placing Cather in the modernist tradition, which evokes sexual experience indirectly, Wasserman stresses the human interest of Cather's fiction as well as its moral and artistic responsibilities. And the same method that creates a sympathetic response to her portrayal of the erotic adumbrates the subtle ways Cather intimates homosexuality.

Cather's aesthetics are inextricably connected with sexuality. As her journalism suggests, Cather perceived the "kingdom of art" as an exclusively male domain. But while the thrust of Cather's early prose endorses a masculine aesthetic, her early fiction tells a different story and shows her in the process of separating creativity from masculinity. Sharon O'Brien considers the personal factors that may have helped Cather question Victorian gender ideology. For instance, Cather's friendship with Sarah Orne Jewett provided her a female mentor and literary model that increased her sympathy toward women writers. Male friends like Ethelbert Nevin, the popular composer of sentimental ballads, also redirected her creative energy. O'Brien suggests that to Cather, Nevin was a "girl-boy" who "encouraged her to appreciate the supposedly feminine values of sensitivity and emotional vulnerability" (EV 263). Cather's gentle father provided a similar model and bequeathed his daughter "a personal, familial resource for questioning the social construction of gender" (EV 16). And the enigmatic figure of Julio, Cather's young Mexican guide in the Southwest, "a primitive version of Ethelbert

Nevin" (Lee 89), also enhanced her creativity. In letters to her friend Elizabeth Shepley Sergeant (12 May 1912, 21 May 1912, and 15 June 1912), Cather glowingly describes Julio as Antinous, old gold, sensuous, and beautiful enough to be an artist's model. Stressing Julio's importance to Cather's creativity, O'Brien writes that "he was an emissary from the sensual Latin races who were at home in the desert, Cather's land of passionate revelation." O'Brien goes on to speculate that Cather's "romance with Julio (like her life and fiction in general) exposes the inadequacy of the categories we generally use—male, female, heterosexual, homosexual, sexual, nonsexual—to describe human experience" (EV 412–13).

Julio is also interesting for the continuity he brings to Cather's pattern of friendships with unusual men. In *Willa Cather: A Critical Biography* E. K. Brown comments that as a girl in Red Cloud, Cather "threw herself impetuously against the way of the majority and sought out the exceptions, the dreamers, the nonconformists, the questioners" (vii)—an early bohemianism reinforcing what James Woodress considers her later "tolerance for a variety of life styles" (LL 236). Julio, Ethelbert Nevin, and even the sophisticated Carl Van Vechten with his "flamboyant knowledge of the world" (Kazin 244) anticipate Cather's later friendships with Truman Capote and Stephen Tennant, two men whose homosexuality was an undeniable part of their unconventionality and uniqueness.[1]

In what ways are these experiences applicable to Cather's imaginative purposes? While Cather's journalism reveals a marked ambivalence toward writers like Wilde and Whitman, early stories like "Jack-a-Boy" (1901) show her exploring the questions these writers raised by emphasizing a creative androgyny. Increasingly, however, the cultural phenomenon of homosexuality, impressed upon Cather through personal observations and literary preferences, engendered another direction in her art.

Perhaps the earliest story to incorporate a homosexual aesthetic into its narrative is "The Tale of the White Pyramid" (1892), a story important not only for its inclusion of homosexuality but also for the particular way Cather treats the subject in comparison to her later handling of the issue. Although O'Brien argues that in her early stories, especially "The Tale of the White Pyramid," Cather attempts both to contain and to draw upon her lesbianism (EV 205), male homosexuality seems a more immediate source of her art. This story also shows Cather's early habit of blending exoticism and eroticism, a characteristic of popular French fiction; both these qualities suffuse "The Tale of the White Pyramid." Its Egyptian setting, for example, resembles Gautier's short story "One of Cleopatra's Nights," which Cather places "among the priceless things of art" (W&P 733). And just as sex animates Gautier's "interminable hieroglyphics" (304), a sexual energy likewise charges the mystery and silence of Cather's story.

Suggestions of homosexuality in "The Tale of the White Pyramid" are surprisingly overt. Describing the Egyptian king and his unpopular young architect of unsurpassed physical beauty, Cather's narrator hints at a sinful relationship about which his "lips are sealed." While the exotic setting and the loaded word "sin" convey the trappings of decadence, male beauty and masculine desire specify homosexuality; and a final image of "the charioteer of the king lash[ing] his horses across the plain toward the city" (CSF 533) unmistakably locates Cather's story in a landscape of homosexual myth and metaphor (Plato's "charioteer" and "the cities of the plain"—Sodom and Gomorrah). Although Mary Ruth Ryder considers the story "unique among the Cather canon for its setting in ancient Egypt," she argues that its "underpinning of mythic images neither sustains nor augments the narrative" (16). However, the subject and its presentation draw attention to Cather's dilemma at the time and strikingly contrast with her subsequent fiction. Here her narrative style is curiously uneven, both direct and indirect, explicitly alluding to the "sin" of the king while simultaneously silencing her narrator. This early story shows Cather exploring a subject for its narrative potential but unsure of its presentation, and, unlike her later unobtrusive handling of homosexuality, "The Tale of the White Pyramid" betrays an obvious effort at disclosure and concealment.

Not until *The Troll Garden* (1905) does Cather move tow/ indirect articulation of homosexuality. Commenting on ' _ Case," Elizabeth Shepley Sergeant observes that Paul was "the first of the young men whom [Cather] was to draw with a special sympathy" (67). If we add the protagonists of "The Sculptor's Funeral" and "A Wagner Matinee" to this list, we begin to perceive a pattern emerging in Cather's early stories and recognize the contribution homosexuality makes to her artistic development.

Initial reviews of *The Troll Garden* condemned it as a lurid and unwholesome "ash-heap of the human mind" that depicted "abnormal" people and freakish psychology (quoted in O'Brien, EV 285). Cather, however, described her stories as "intangible impressions and moods" (quoted in EV 281). Amid these delicate feelings, homosexuality becomes a unifying element in Cather's design. That Cather republished "Paul's Case," "The Sculptor's Funeral," and "A Wagner Matinee" in 1920 and again in the signature edition of her works in 1937 further underscores this pattern and forces attention to the significance of her early stories regarding not merely her art but also, as Roger Austen suggests, the development of gay American literature:

> At first glance it appears that "Paul's Case" and "The Sculptor's Funeral" (both 1905) have no connection with overt homosexuality, but on closer reading both stories provide an unflinching look at the stifling conditions that sent sensitive young men from the smaller towns and cities of mid-America into the havens of the big cities at the turn of the century. While not all of these young men were gay, some of them undoubtedly were, and Cather has shown with photographic realism the drab ugliness that must have been beyond endurance for the homosexual adolescents who were unlucky enough to have been born and raised in a provincial environment. (PG 31–32)

Since its publication "Paul's Case" has become Cather's most recognizable short fiction; likewise, it has gradually emerged as her representative gay text. In fact, it has become something of a critical commonplace to read homosexuality in the story, and in doing so, critics have discovered the indirect manner in which Cather treats the subject as well as the contributions it makes to her art. Larry Rubin first identified a homosexual motif in "Paul's Case" in 1975, paying close attention to the manner in which it moves the story away from the clinical aura of a case study toward subtle, psychological portraiture. Rubin collects what he considers to be clues to Paul's sexual nature, such as his physical appearance, social relationships, personal habits, and inner feelings, all of which, he stresses, indirectly hint at "Paul's deviation from what the culture of [Cather's] day . . . would consider the sexual norm" (129). Specific examples in the story include Paul's theatrically expressive eyes, "remarkable for a certain hysterical brilliancy . . . peculiarly offensive in a boy" (TTG 102), his use of violet water, friendships with boys his own age or slightly older, and an "apprehensive dread" of "the thing in the corner" (114). Particularly interesting among these suggestive details is Paul's encounter with the "wild" (117) freshman from Yale. As they embark upon a night on the town together, their relationship is cordial; their parting in the morning, however, is "singularly cool" (117)—an event that leaves the reader, as Rubin suggests, "with an unshakable sense of innuendo" (130).

Such details build a convincing argument for Paul's unstated sexuality. But homosexuality does more in "Paul's Case" than describe its protagonist's nature, and it is here that readers begin to feel the effects of Cather's sexual aesthetics. Rubin explains:

> The importance of all this for a balanced critical evaluation of the story lies not so much in the fact that Paul is very probably homosexual by nature and temperament, but that Cather is trying to show us the tragic consequences of the conflict between a sensitive and hence alienated temperament, on the one hand, and a narrowly "moral," bourgeois environment, on the other. It is one of her more familiar themes, and has been widely dealt with by critics; but here it would seem important to be aware of the homosexuality of the

sensitive protagonist in order to comprehend the full depth of his alienation from the "normal" American society in which he feels trapped and hence the full pathos of his situation. (131)

Cather's subtle treatment of homosexuality in this early story intensifies her skill at narrative indirection and positions "Paul's Case" more securely with her mature work than with her apprentice fiction.

Building upon Rubin's observations, Claude J. Summers sees homosexuality in "Paul's Case" as more than simply a metaphor for alienation. He places the story in the forefront of modern gay fiction and argues that its homosexual aspects enable Cather to make a powerful social commentary. As Rubin distances "Paul's Case" from the clinical and criminal implications of its title, Summers begins his argument by emphasizing the sexual connotations of its subtitle, "A Study in Temperament."[2] Extending Rubin's list of sexual clues, Summers stresses the subliminal impact of Cather's language:

> Throughout the story, Cather repeatedly uses diction suggestive of homosexuality. Although in almost every instance the words are used with no specific allusion to homosexuality, the startling number and pervasiveness of such terms as *gay* (used four times), *fairy, faggot, fagged, queen, loitering, tormented, unnatural, haunted, different, perverted, secret love,* and so forth create a verbal ambiance that subtly but persistently calls attention to the issue. However innocently used, these words and phrases appear too often to be merely coincidental. They function to help establish the overtone by which the ear divines homosexuality in the text. (*Gay Fictions* 67)

Summers goes beyond the surface details of the story to reveal its symbolic importance that for him lies in Cather's response to Oscar Wilde—his life, his trial, and his posthumous *De Profundis.* For Summers, "The reaction of the teachers to Paul parallels Cather's own excessive reaction to Wilde's mocking manner in the 1890's, and may reflect the author's mature reconsideration of her own earlier lack of imagination in not dealing charitably with Wilde in his disgrace" (69). Consequently, "Paul's Case" becomes both an indictment of Wildean aestheticism and an alternative to its limitations.

Paul is Cather's Wildean aesthete. His dandified appearance, his "scandalous red carnation" (TTG 103), and his loathing of the commonplace associate him with what Cather perceived to be the negative attributes of aestheticism. Most damning, however, Paul lacks sympathy for others. In criticizing Paul's deficiency, Cather strongly indicts the aesthetic movement for its lack of imagination, but rather than the position Wilde offers in *De Profundis*, which calls for the homosexual to reject society, Cather advocates human sympathy. Summers finds this implicit in the optimistic motto "Feed my Lambs" (TTG 107), which "haunts the story as an unnamed presence that promises the possibility of integrating outcasts like Paul—and like Wilde and other homosexuals—into the community, and doing so without violating their individuality" (*Gay Fictions* 74). Although O'Brien sees Cather still subordinating herself to the male tradition in "Paul's Case," part of the story's maturity is its questioning of masculine ideals, and important in this social critique is Oscar Wilde's role in helping Cather convey the need for diversity and acceptance. "As a gay fiction," Summers writes, "'Paul's Case' is complex and resonant. . . . subtly implying alternatives to alienation and suicide and envisioning possibilities implicit in those homilies by which the world is run" (76).

By envisioning alternatives, Cather's story breaks with the obligatory treatment of homosexuality, which prescribes death or prolonged despair. Homosexuality in "Paul's Case" is not the reason for Paul's tragedy, and his suicide is not the stereotypical tragic ending for gay characters. Rather, as Summers explains, the cause of Paul's unhappiness and suicide is "his inability to integrate his homosexuality into real life" (*Gay Fictions* 68). The subject of homosexuality thus allows Cather poignantly to dramatize her appeal for human sympathy, which is necessary in life and in art.

Gay readings such as Rubin's and Summers's extend our understanding of "Paul's Case" and the complexities of Cather's art.

They also provide interpretative models for looking at other stories to see how homosexuality shapes Cather's aesthetics. Alice Hall Petry, for instance, finds homosexuality to be the dominant theme of "The Sculptor's Funeral" and writes that Cather's story is "a remarkably astute study of a family, a town, a society failing to come to terms, not with a young man's artistic inclinations, but rather his homosexuality" (108–09).

As with "Paul's Case," Cather does not mention homosexuality directly in "The Sculptor's Funeral," yet its presence is felt throughout the narrative. Petry argues that Harvey Merrick's homosexuality "is evident in the story's opening scene" (109) and supports this interpretation with a variety of telling clues. Cather's description of the group of people assembled to meet the train that is bringing Merrick's body home—their speech, conduct, body language, and the conspicuous absence of family and friends—emphasizes their discomfort at being associated with Merrick. The uneasiness of their situation is climaxed by one member's disavowal of being Merrick's "friend"—a word linked, as Petry points out, to a sexual partner. Petry also finds suggestive details in Merrick's home and family, especially the "sexual confusion" (111) of his parents that would cause Merrick to reject heterosexual love. In their house hangs a print of John Alden and Priscilla—as Petry says, "the first famous heterosexual couple in the annals of America" (110); it is an icon that intensifies the reader's understanding of Henry Steavens's mistake in having placed his friend's coffin beneath it.

By delineating personal relationships in "The Sculptor's Funeral," homosexual innuendo once again demonstrates Cather's sympathetic imagination. For Petry, "it is the rather elusive relationship between Merrick, Steavens, and Laird which constitutes one of the most intriguing aspects of the story" (113). In explaining the town's collective hostility, she argues that their cold reception of Steavens manifests their suspicion of a previously sexual relationship between the sculptor and his student, "their instinctive belief that whoever accompanied the body from Boston—that hotbed of dubious relations between persons of the same sex, made famous by Henry James's *The Bostonians* (1886)—would quite likely be of the same sexual inclinations as the sculptor" (112).

An image of Harvey Merrick emerges from conversational remarks about him, a complex portrait colored by the blurring of homosexual and artistic inclinations. Petry observes that "in fact it is unclear whether the men of Sand City cannot, or simply will not, articulate their uneasiness about Merrick's homosexuality. They speak of it as a disinclination for practical matters . . . and they associate it insistently with Merrick's artistic temperament" (114). Comments of the townspeople supply information about Merrick such as "his ladylike voice" (TTG 41) and impracticality; conversation between Laird and Steavens provides other details, such as his gentleness, kindness, and sensitivity. And while Laird's description of the young sculptor's preference for a prairie sunset over the profits of a farm reveals both an aesthetic temperament and a defiance of convention, Petry adds that the lawyer's impassioned defense is perhaps "less Laird's tolerance of Harvey's 'impractical' artistic sensibilities than his knowledge and acceptance of Merrick's sexual preferences" (113).

"A Wagner Matinee" continues Cather's exploration of human sympathy in *The Troll Garden*. Susan J. Rosowski sees it as "the story of the narrator's awakening humanity" (VP 27) as Clark moves from first observing his aunt with cold objectivity to his later feeling of genuine compassion. Although sexuality in the story is subordinated to its focus on sympathy, Wasserman connects all three stories to a philosophical call to beauty. Consequently, her discussion of Plato's "ladder of love" announces Cather's emerging platonic paradigm and uncovers the oblique contribution homosexuality makes to the stories' cumulative theme of "the indestructibility of the soul that knows beauty" ("Is Cather's Paul?" 128). Wagner's music is an appropriate choice to evoke this theme, for its connection with the homosexual imagination has long been felt. As Byrne Fone summarizes, "Wagner's lyrical praise of physical masculine beauty echoes earlier Greek poetry and combines the themes of physical beauty, masculine love, and friendship, with prowess in battle, themes common to Wagner's work as well as to German romanticism, and derived clearly from the Greeks" (HH 72).

Cather's concern for sympathy continues as the focus of her fiction shifts from the world of art to that of human relationships. While *O Pioneers!* (1913) recognizes human differences, *My Ántonia* (1918) presents the struggle for self-identity, and in both novels Cather's treatment of homosexuality refines the technical and thematic complexities begun in *The Troll Garden*. "Except for some of the people who lived in it, I think no one had ever found Nebraska beautiful until Willa Cather wrote about it," recalls Edith Lewis in *Willa Cather Living* (17).[3] Just as Cather makes Nebraska compelling in her fiction, so too does she make homosexuality a compelling aspect of her narratives, and *O Pioneers!* is her first novel to engender respect for both of these achievements.

With its title borrowed from Walt Whitman and its dedication to Sarah Orne Jewett, *O Pioneers!* opens in recognition of diversity. Its epigraph—"Those fields, colored by various grain!"—links this theme to the landscape that inspires it; for, indeed, if the land is the "great fact" (15) in *O Pioneers!*, it is also the novel's all-embracing metaphor.[4] Sexual diversity enlarges these patterns of differences in *O Pioneers!*, and homosexuality, in particular, enters into their configurations.[5] Whitman and Jewett not only represent diverse literary traditions but point as well to something inherent in Cather's own fiction, a shared respect for same-sex friendships. Consequently, Cather's acknowledged predecessors are emblematic of more than male and female literary inheritances or virile spontaneity coupled with delicate restraint: they embody a unique relationship between friendship and creativity and bestow to Cather's art a legacy of the spiritual potential of personal relations.

Cather invigorates the early episodes of *O Pioneers!* with the vitality of male friendship. As boys, Emil Bergson and Amédée Chevalier are inseparable. Wrestling, riding, larking together, frequently "arm in arm" (163), they blend the masculine affection found in the novels of Pierre Loti with the athletic exuberance of Whitman's "Calamus" poems. Cather's form and content also unite to classically sanction male friendship. As Hermione Lee points out, Cather's reference to "'jumping and wrestling and throwing the discus' . . . turn[s] a Nebraskan baseball game into an Olympiad" (115), thus Hellenizing Cather's "two-part pastoral."

Boyhood friendship changes as Emil and Amédée enter the world of adult sexuality, and just as homosexual imagery brightens the early episodes of O Pioneers!, so too does it develop the novel's later tension. Emil's bohemian interlude in Mexico City affects a decadent pose, and later in the novel, homosexual innuendo overtly surfaces. Boasting of his new-found happiness as husband and father, Amédée expresses bewilderment at Emil's coolness to-ward the French girls and asks his friend if he is "stuck up" or if he intends to be a priest; more pointedly, he asks Emil, "is anything the matter with you?" (160–61) that he does not have a sweetheart. Even Emil's fellow students had observed "something queer" (180) about the handsome Swede. While the word *queer* can be a com-monplace expression, by the early twentieth century it had ac-quired connotations of sexual deviancy. Cather's frequent use of the term enhances the ambiguity of her language and brings to her narratives a verbal aura of the unusual and unconventional.

To present Emil's unhappiness Cather characteristically turns to landscape imagery, and here too homosexual innuendo evokes powerful feelings. Her image of two seeds planted side by side— one shooting up joyfully, the other rotting inexplicably in the ground—is a particularly mournful metaphor. While Emil "liked to see and to think about Amédée's sunny, natural, happy love" (163), his love for the married Marie Shabata remains hidden and repressed. Cather's faint suggestion of its unnaturalness surpasses the narrative context of Emil's frustration and sharpens the poign-ancy of her image. While Emil is clearly meant to be heterosexual, the Housman-like aura of homosexuality surrounding Cather's characterization suggestively colors his feelings and conveys his despair.

Characterizations further extend Cather's landscape imagery into human relationships. To stress Alexandra's autonomy, the narrator first describes the impressive prosperity of the Bergson farm and afterward adds that "the farmer was a woman, Alexandra Bergson" (83). Such gender specificity leads a reader to wonder: if Cather's women are the farmers, what then are her men? As if to answer that question, Cather creates Carl Linstrum. Throughout *O Pioneers!* Cather describes Carl by images of gender ambiguity embellished with homosexual overtones, a blurring process that unmistakably identifies him as an unconventional male. While *unconventional* and *homosexual* are not synonymous terms, homosexual innuendo can be an effective strategy by which to stress unconventionality; the converse can also be true. Lonely, sensitive, and artistic, absorbed in dreaming and drawing, every detail about Carl distances him from other males such as Lou and Oscar Bergson and the traditional definitions of masculinity they embody and links him more closely with earlier protagonists like Paul and Harvey Merrick.

Carl's very differences characterize his strength, a strength admired by Alexandra and Cather alike. In consoling Alexandra after the deaths of Emil and Marie, Carl displays a heightened sensibility: "My dear, it was something one felt in the air, as you feel the spring coming, or a storm in summer. I did n't *see* anything. Simply, when I was with those two young things, I felt my blood go quicker, I felt—how shall I say it?—an acceleration of life. After I got away, it was all too delicate, too intangible, to write about" (305). Carl's intense introspection and self-consciousness broaden into human sympathy. While not unique to homosexuals, a rigorous observation of the self and society is often the consequence when one is different from the norm—a sensitivity is developed that can make homosexuals, like artists, keen observers of the world around them (Kellogg 7).[6] In describing his feelings about Emil and Marie, Carl uses language similar to Alexandra's appeal to her brothers after returning from the river country, her intuitive trust in the future of the land. This similarity in language reveals shared sympathies as well. Able to read the landscape, Alexandra learns from Carl to read human emotions; she grows in human sympathy, and her realization at the end of the novel "that we are not all made alike" (305) returns the narrative to its opening recognition of diversity.

Walt Whitman, Sarah Orne Jewett, A. E. Housman, and Pierre Loti, even Walter Pater, are all part of Cather's narrative landscape, an allusive density swelling into metaphor.[7] Now a new, and perhaps unexpected, landmark appears—Oscar Wilde. Coming after her visit to the State Penitentiary in Lincoln, Alexandra's epiphany calls to mind Wilde's imprisonment; indeed, prisons and imprisonment are among Cather's most recurring metaphors, especially in the texts I am examining. Seen in this context, Wilde becomes an influence upon Cather's imagination different from what has previously been thought. He brings with him a homosexual aesthetic that Cather evokes in the very substance and texture of the novel so central to her canon.[8]

Rather than creating a central Wildean figure as in "Paul's Case," Cather diffuses Wilde-like characteristics among several characters. Emil, Carl, and Frank all manifest mannerisms associated with Oscar Wilde—Emil's bohemian pose and exotic costumes and Carl's sensitivity and artistic longing, for example. Curiously, Cather gives Frank Shabata, perhaps her least Wilde-like character, her strongest Wildean treatment. His striking appearance recalls the familiar image of Wilde the dandy: "He was easily the buck of the beer-gardens, and on Sunday he was a sight to see, with his silk hat and tucked shirt and blue frock-coat, wearing gloves and carrying a little wisp of a yellow cane. He was tall and fair, with splendid teeth and close-cropped yellow curls, and he wore a slightly disdainful expression, proper for a young man with high connections, whose mother had a big farm in the Elbe valley" (143). Rings, gloves, and walking sticks are all accessories for aesthetic posturing, such as Frank's "love-lorn attitudes" (146) and "way of drawing out his cambric handkerchief slowly, by one corner, from his breast-pocket, that was melancholy and romantic in the extreme" (144). In *The Wilde Century: Effeminacy, Oscar Wilde and the Queer Moment*, Alan Sinfield points out the fluidity of terms like *aesthetics, decadence, effeminacy,* and *dandy,* all of which, he believes, "trembl[e] on the brink of homosexuality" (93). While similar sensibilities suffuse *O Pioneers!,* the prison scene clearly establishes Frank's Wildean identity and reveals Cather's strongest affinity with the "High Priest of the Decadents" (Ellmann 475).

No prisoner was more famous at the turn of the century than Oscar Wilde. Convicted in 1895 of "acts of gross indecency with another male," he was sentenced to two years of hard labor, most of which he spent at Reading Gaol. If, as Summers argues, the importance of "Paul's Case" lies in Cather's changed response to Wilde, *O Pioneers!* continues this reconciliation.[9] And it is, I believe, Alexandra's visit to Frank Shabata in prison that dramatically reveals Wilde's influence on Cather's imagination. Rosowski writes that Cather creates sympathy for Frank through subtleties of style and language, "mak[ing] the case that he deserves Alexandra's—and the reader's—compassion" ("Adaptations" 140). Prisoners as well as pioneers thus enact Cather's redemptive drama; ironically, in her first major novel, as in her first major short story, her sympathy and sympathetic imagination are linked to Oscar Wilde.

Wilde himself visited the State Penitentiary in Lincoln, Nebraska, on 24 April 1882 while on his American lecture tour. It was the first prison he had ever been inside, and it made a lasting impression.[10] Richard Ellmann describes Wilde's visit: "He exhibited a childlike faith in physiognomy. On being shown photographs of some of the convicts, he commented, 'O, what a dreadful face. And what did he do?' Warden Nobes did not hesitate to tell of the criminals in the most graphic manner. 'Oh, here's a beast, an animal,' exclaimed Wilde of one picture, 'nothing of the man left'" (201). Wilde's observations correspond in interesting ways with Alexandra's later visit. Alexandra, too, is visiting a prison for the first time, and for both the place is horrifying. Unlike Wilde, however, Alexandra refuses the warden's invitation to "go through the institution" (298). As Wilde had studied pictures of numerous inmates, Alexandra focuses intently on Frank Shabata: "Alexandra was bewildered. Frank seemed to have undergone a change of personality.

There was scarcely anything by which she could recognize her handsome Bohemian neighbor. He seemed, somehow, not altogether human. She did not know what to say to him" (294). While waiting for Frank, Alexandra pays close attention to another prisoner, "a pale young man in convicts' clothes" (291), whose description seems almost a reincarnation of Wilde himself:

> The warden's clock ticked, the young convict's pen scratched busily in the big book, and his sharp shoulders were shaken every few seconds by a loose cough which he tried to smother. It was easy to see that he was a sick man. Alexandra looked at him timidly, but he did not once raise his eyes. He wore a white shirt under his striped jacket, a high collar, and a necktie, very carefully tied. His hands were thin and white and well cared for, and he had a seal ring on his little finger. When he heard steps approaching in the corridor, he rose, blotted his book, put his pen in the rack, and left the room without raising his eyes. (291–92)

Such details conflate a variety of related events—Wilde's and Frank's imprisonments as well as Alexandra's and Wilde's visits to the Lincoln Penitentiary. We can add to these correspondences the visits made to Wilde in prison by his friends and supporters, whose accounts describe his declining health ("shattered by fatigue," "malnourished," "depressed," "emaciated," an "absolute wreck") as well as his reading and writing habits (see Ellmann 479–524).

From this confluence of prison imagery, yet another connection is possible. Alexandra's trips away from the Divide are important for what she discovers while gone. After visiting the river country, she returns home in a joyous mood, humming an old Swedish hymn. Returning from Lincoln, a more somber Alexandra remembers

> some lines from a poem [Byron's "The Prisoner of Chillon"] she had liked in her schooldays:—
> "Henceforth the world will only be / A wider prison-house to me,—" (OP 298)

Like Wilde's life of perpetual exile after his release from prison, Alexandra now envisions a life of inescapable loneliness and isolation.

But Wilde discovers in *De Profundis* that "the secret of life is suffering" (75) and, in having done so, is able to move from pain to consolation. Reunited with Carl, Alexandra is also consoled. Their relationship typifies the values Cather attaches to friendship as it is based on love and sympathy, hallmarks of the comfort that friends can bring to a marriage. And it is by engendering a respect for differences that Cather envisions renewed human relations. Describing Cather's imagination, Guy Reynolds writes that "she was unusually receptive to *difference*, weaving into her novels a broadminded acceptance of the foreign or the strange" (WCIC 16). In *O Pioneers!* this receptivity demonstrates Cather's emerging creative process. As her characters learn to look with love at one another and the land around them, so too does Cather respond with sympathy to her native fields. Cather always insisted that, right or wrong, the country was her hero, and she submitted to this feeling, an unconventionality yielding fortunate results. Likewise, sexual aesthetics further augment the uniqueness of *O Pioneers!* and sustain its singular mood. Cather's acknowledgment that with *O Pioneers!* she "hit the home pasture" (quoted in Bennett 200–01) implicitly recognizes homosexuality's contribution to that discovery and its creative potential.[11]

My Ántonia continues this recognition. As the event is recounted in the introduction to the novel's first edition, Jim Burden brings a manuscript of his reminiscences of Ántonia to his editor friend at her New York apartment. "'Read it as soon as you can,' he said, rising, 'but don't let it influence your own story'" (xiv). Although Cather later deleted this passage, its implications remain intact— readers are urged to see Ántonia for themselves and, like Jim Burden, to create their own story. Cather's intriguing introduction to *My Ántonia* also alerts readers to the multiplicity of choices facing an imaginative writer. The introduction's revisions underscore both its connections with the story it begins and the affinities it suggests between the homosexual imagination and literary tradition.

In response to Jim Burden's query about his friend's manuscript, "Now what about yours?" (xiii), Cather's narrator muses, "My own story was never written, but the following narrative is Jim's manuscript, substantially as he brought it to me" (xiv). This passage, later deleted from the introduction, closely resembles the narrative strategy of Xavier Mayne's *Imre: A Memorandum* (1906), considered to be the first openly gay and affirmative novel written by an American (although published abroad). In its preface the narrator implies that he is not really the author but merely the editor of a manuscript sent to him by a British friend. Pierre Loti's *Mon frère Yves* anticipates another strategy Cather uses in *My Ántonia*. After inserting seemingly incidental and unrelated details about his subject, Loti's narrator parenthetically explains his decisions: "I cannot say that this has any connection with my story of Yves; I merely set down what has chanced to remain impressed on my memory" (121), a narrative choice similar to Jim Burden's invocation of memory in writing about Ántonia. That *My Ántonia* so curiously resembles these two important gay texts suggests not so much specific literary sources as it does the spirit of affiliation between Cather's fiction and the homosexual literary tradition, a kinship shaping alike not only their stories but also the way those stories are told and interpreted. Like the pastoral form in *O Pioneers!*, rich in homosexual associations, this nexus of gay texts introducing *My Ántonia* introduces as well its ambiguous sexual identities.[12]

Such narrative license as the novel's introduction allows invites an unusual degree of interpretative freedom, and responses have been particularly inventive concerning sexuality in the novel. While Lee calls *My Ántonia* "a very sexy book" (154), other critics go further and specify a variety of sexualities the text engages. For instance, Judith Fetterley's interpretation of *My Ántonia* as a lesbian novel rejects arguments such as Woodress's that "there is no evidence from the fiction that Cather's sexual preference influenced her writing" and that "In her novels and stories she is completely androgynous" ("Cather and Her Friends" 84). In Fetterley's view, Cather was forced to emotionally distance herself from her narrative but was at the same time unable to totally renounce her love of women. In particular, says Fetterley, Cather's sensual description of Lena Lingard shows "the strength of her resistance to renouncing her lesbian sensibility" (159). Fetterley further observes that the narrative's textual act is itself lesbian, uniting the muse not with a Virgilian *patria* but rather, in Cather's case, a "matria," a female landscape "safely eroticized and safely loved" (161).[13]

Like lesbianism, male homosexuality heightens the ambiguity of *My Ántonia*, and in turn this ambiguity intensifies Cather's treatment of homosexuality. Since Brown first identified an emotional emptiness at the heart of *My Ántonia* (202), readers and critics have sought to fill that void. Brown attributes this emptiness to Cather's conflicting motives in adopting a male narrator. "Jim was to be fascinated by Ántonia as only a man could be," Brown writes, "and yet he was to remain a detached observer, appreciative but inactive, rather than take a part in her life" (202). Intimations of homosexuality reduce the incompatibility of these narrative demands by revealing other possibilities. Jim's passivity, his detached admiration of the hired girls, his "queer" (246) adolescent habits, his lack of interest in marrying Ántonia, and his seemingly loveless New York marriage become less problematic when read as expressions of a homosexual temperament. Rather than empty, Jim and Ántonia's relationship represents another recognition on Cather's part of the range of personal relations based on friendship.[14]

As they do in the novel's introduction, gay literary affinities support these readings. In *O Pioneers!* Carl Linstrum fits the nineteenth-century concept of *Uranianism*, a term derived from Plato's *Symposium* and used by early sexologists to define homosexuality. Later, it took on a more specific meaning, designating boy-love in particular. A literary movement of Uranian poets grew up around this phenomenon and flourished from the 1890s to the 1930s. Works by men like John Gambril Nicholson, E. E. Bradford, and

Charles Kains-Jackson frequently appeared in such English journals as the *Spirit Lamp*, edited by Lord Alfred Douglas, and the *Artist and Journal of Home Culture*.[15]

While Cather's familiarity with these writers is not documented, her avid reading during her college years, her magazine work from 1896 through 1912, her trips to England, and her alertness to new literary material would have placed her in a knowledgeable position. Her own interest in Uranian themes would also have made her a sympathetic reader (the earlier story "Jack-a-Boy," for instance, about the transforming effects a young boy has upon the residents of Windsor Terrace, exudes the language of Uranianism—"Patroclus," "Pater," "Greeks," "gay," and so on). A recent anthology of Uranian verse offers an overview of the social milieu in which much of this poetry was written:

> The Oscar Wilde persecution was fresh in people's minds, it was an era of militaristic heterosexual tyranny and most importantly the time of the mass carnage of the first World War. The loss of friends and lovers, the witnessing of untold bloodshed and brutality, and the circumspect way in which gay relationships and liaisons were conducted resulted in a specific sensibility. One in which death was ever present, ceremony and pageant provided much needed meaning and the nostalgia of idealized boyhood provided an escape from the hostile straight world. (Webb n. pag.)

My Ántonia, published in 1918, seems oddly removed from such events, yet beneath its calm surface it shares many of the concerns of the Uranian poets. Specifically, the haymow scene near the end of the novel, where Jim frolics with Ántonia's young sons, is perhaps the most tantalizing in this connection. Observing the boys at play, Jim records that "they tickled each other and tossed and tumbled in the hay; and then, all at once, as if they had been shot, they were still. There was hardly a minute between giggles and bland slumber" (341). This intruding image, "as if they had been shot," coupled with the novel's insistent focus on death, punctures the serenity and detachment of Cather's text. Could the "shooting" of

Ántonia's sons be as much an indictment of World War I as it is a further demonstration of Jim's rifle fixation? I am not suggesting here that Jim either is or is not homosexual; rather, by placing the scene in a Uranian context, I am showing how Cather draws upon a "specific sensibility" to shape her fiction as well as to form her social critique.[16]

Uranian sentiments, of course, surface in all great artists, from Michelangelo and Caravaggio to Whitman and Housman. While Cather is no exception, especially in her idealization of youth and boyhood, seldom has this theme played such a strategic part in one of her narratives. Cather stresses its importance with the section title "Cuzak's Boys," an echo of the "boys' books" she so admired— texts like *Kidnapped* and *Treasure Island* that "introduced homosexual desire under the guise of boyish escapism" (Koestenbaum, DT 144). And it is interesting too that in writing his reminiscences, Jim not only is the observer of boys—as is, for instance, the artist Henry Scott Tuke, who achieved fame as the painter of local youths near his home in Falmouth, Cornwall—but also places himself in the scene, as does Thomas Eakins in his painting *The Swimming Hole* (see Cooper 33–42). Through homoerotic imagery, Cather is thus able to invest Jim's nostalgia with a poignant sense of urgency, sympathetic to the popular sentimentalism of "The Old Oaken Bucket" yet subverting it at the same time with narrative affiliations to the Uranian poets.[17]

While Jim Burden may not be conventionally male, neither is he convincingly female. Rather, he is a complex individual, "an androgynous narrator who mediates between male and female worlds" (Lee 153). And it is precisely this type of androgyny and gender ambiguity seen in the protagonists of Cather's early fiction that leads one to an exploration of homosexuality in her later, male-centered novels. Adding that Jim "is both boyish and girlish" (154), Lee describes an even more complex pattern of duality in Cather's art, for the engendering of Cather's fiction coincides with the emerging of her voice.

4

The Greek
Ideal in *One of Ours*

CATHER'S intimations of homosexuality in her
early fiction expand into a more fully realized treatment of the subject in the 1920s. In a way the focus of her male-centered novels
during this period becomes a narrative response to her familiar
statement that "The world broke in two in 1922 or thereabouts"
(*Not Under Forty* v). Examining Cather's attempts "to weld her
world whole again" (10), Merrill Maguire Skaggs emphasizes her
"continuing concentration on her chosen personal material and
her consistent willingness to consider that material from more
than one angle" (28). The creation of a homosexual paradigm in
One of Ours, The Professor's House, and *Death Comes for the Archbishop* is one such distinctive narration. Consistent with her pattern
of inverting her material or changing important variables, Cather
now shifts the focus at the heart of *O Pioneers!* and *My Ántonia* to a
concentration on male friendship, through which she continues to
explore the spiritual potential of human relations.

In addition to reflecting the narrative importance she attaches to
homosexuality at this time, Cather's paradigm also heightens the
spiritual kinship among her works of fiction. Commenting on the
emotional and thematic unity of Cather's texts, Edward A. and Lil-

lian D. Bloom write that "As is true of any serious novelist, she worked toward broad relationships among her novels and she tended to limit her field of vision to achieve that purpose" (175). Skaggs further describes this interconnectedness: "any item that helps one to grasp a nuance in a single Cather novel is likely to re-appear as a help in another novel as well. Cather's work has a con-tinuity in which symbols and themes and techniques repeatedly re-surface. . . . Some dialogues, arguments, or explorations extend through several books" (14). Although they are separate narratives, *One of Ours*, *The Professor's House*, and *Death Comes for the Arch-bishop* manifest this continuity and acquire composite meaning through Cather's treatment of homosexuality. Indeed, attention to this theme gives these texts an identity within the Cather canon comparable to Shakespeare's sonnets and Whitman's "Calamus" poems.

While the fictional settings of these novels—the military, the school, and the church—enhance the subject of male friendship and masculine desire, Cather's evocation of homosexuality extends beyond the surface details of her fiction. In her attempt to "allego-rize" (Edward and Lillian Bloom 79) her protagonists' quest for a meaningful life, Cather recreates homosexuality's most inspiring legend, the Sacred Band of Thebes. Nothing in gay literature or history exerts as strong an imaginative appeal as ancient Greece's army of lovers. Like her excitement over "Hellenic" poets such as Walt Whitman and Bliss Carman (*Songs from Vagabondia*, 1894), Cather's evocation of the Sacred Band intensifies her enthusiasm for a specifically Greek ideal. As Vern L. Bullough writes, "If Plato represents one aspect of Greek thought, it seems that at least cer-tain segments in Greek society found the most characteristic and noble form of love in the passionate friendship between men, or more precisely between the adult male and an adolescent one" (103). In military history this ideal "was perhaps realized in the fourth century in the elite fighting corps at Thebes formed by Gorgidas known as the Sacred Band and consisting of 300 men tra-ditionally grouped as pairs of lovers. The band, admired throughout the Greek world, was responsible for the brief period of military supremacy of Thebes" (106).

Classical references to the Sacred Band consist chiefly of those in Plato, who philosophically advocates the heroic possibilities of an army of lovers, and in Plutarch, who records its actual military history.[1] Modern references to the Sacred Band, however, appear so often in gay literature and history that Stuart Kellogg identifies a tendency among homosexual writers to invoke at some point the Theban band of warriors "as if to exonerate homosexuality by calling on its saints" (6). In the nineteenth century Whitman connects "adhesiveness" with the homosexual idealism of the Sacred Band. For instance, while in "For You O Democracy" he envisions a "continent indissoluble," "inseparable cities," and a land made "divine" by "the life-long love of comrades" (LG 117), Robert K. Martin detects possible references to the Sacred Band in "When I Peruse the Conquered Fame of Heroes" that emphasize Whitman's conviction that "love and fidelity are the highest rewards of life" (HT 79). Likewise, in his poem "Love and Death" (1878) John Addington Symonds alludes to the Sacred Band and links it to such virtues as comradeship, chivalry, and holiness—his warrior-lovers Cratinus and Aristodemus, for example, sacrificing their lives and love for the sake of Athenian liberty. Interestingly, a modified army of lovers appears in *Salammbô*, Flaubert's imaginative reconstruction of ancient Carthage that was Cather's favorite among his novels. As Evelyn Haller writes, "In *Salammbô* the only true instances of sweetly domesticated love are found among the homosexual bondings of mercenary soldiers" (50), and she points out that Cather transmutes this particular love into general human kindness as exemplified by the friendship between Hallet and Cesarino in her story "Behind the Singer Tower" (1912).

Finding truth in a classical ideal, Cather embodies that truth in her rendition of the Sacred Band. But as Greek thought faded with the spread of Christianity, so too did Cather's novels follow this historical shift from classical sanctions of homosexuality to Christian restraint. It is no coincidence that *One of Ours* is Cather's most overtly homoerotic novel while *Death Comes for the Archbishop* is her most celibate. A gay reading suggests Cather's narrative design: the search for the ideal friend in *One of Ours* leads to the idealized friendship of *Death Comes for the Archbishop*. Set between the two, *The Professor's House* reflects a transitional moment of historical and cultural awareness. As Symonds wrote, "The transmutation of Hellas proper into part of the Roman Empire, and the intrusion of Stoicism and Christianity into the sphere of Hellenic thought and feeling, mark the end of the Greek age" (80). For Godfrey St. Peter a similar transition marks the end of delight, and in *The Professor's House* Cather despairingly looks at life without the friend or the lasting friendship.

Although Cather continues to evoke homosexuality, her texts continually transcend it. To achieve platonic fulfillment, Cather fuses eros and agape. Of Cather's novels of the twenties and early thirties, Elizabeth Shepley Sergeant writes that "Their significance tends to the religious" (193), and Bernice Slote adds that it was inevitable that Cather would attempt to "return a little of the kingdom of art to the kingdom of heaven, from which it came" ("First Principles" 111). Homosexuality contains eternal truths, and Cather's art of friendship allegorically assists in their recovery. Beginning in the physical and ending in the spiritual, Cather's platonic paradigm thus becomes the paradigm of art itself, "the human ritual of the discovery of the divine" (Slote, "First Principles" 49). As her Sacred Band moves from an army of lovers to the love of friends, Cather's sexual aesthetics enact this imaginative journey.[2]

. . .

Early in her journalistic career Willa Cather acknowledged that "a book is precious to me for what it means to me, not for what it means to cleverer persons than I" (W&P 362). In 1925, looking back over her published fiction, Cather reaffirmed this attitude when she selected *One of Ours* (1922) as the book she liked best of all her novels and the one with the most "value" in it (Bohlke 78). Ironically, Cather's Pulitzer Prize–winning novel has received the harshest criticism of any of her fiction, and its value eludes many readers.

On the surface *One of Ours* seems to be a war novel, its final two sections placing its protagonist in the trenches of France during World War I and its first three sections preparing him for that destination. On these terms *One of Ours* has been traditionally read and often judged a failure, a dismissal perpetuated by Ernest Hemingway's disparagement of its climactic ending: "E. E. Cummings' *Enormous Room* was the best book published last year that I read. Somebody told me it was a flop. Then look at *One of Ours*. Prize, big sale, people taking it seriously. You were in the war weren't you? Wasn't that last scene in the lines wonderful? Do you know where it came from? The battle scene in *Birth of a Nation*. I identified episode after episode, Catherized. Poor woman she had to get her war experience somewhere" (105). But as Skaggs has written, "The central fact about *One of Ours* that one must see in order to read it intelligently at all is that the book is bathed and saturated in irony" (40). The novel's chief irony is that it is more about love and friendship than it is about war. Hermione Lee further argues that "If all that the novel were doing was presenting a heroic picture of 'our' noble American boys sacrificing themselves at the front for an ideal, then Mencken's and Hemingway's attacks on the novel would have to be the last word" (172). The appearance of Cather's "The Novel Démeublé" in the *Atlantic Monthly* the same year the novel was published encourages readers to look beyond the surface story and ask what is "the thing not named" in *One of Ours*?

Scholarship on *One of Ours* suggests answers to this question. While Alfred Kazin sees the novel as the "proverbial story of the sensitive young man" (253), other critics explore the diverse contexts of that archetype. Susan J. Rosowski interprets *One of Ours* as "an American version of Arthurian legend" (VP 97), of a wandering knight in search of a chivalric ideal; she identifies literary parallels with Keats and Tennyson. Stanley Cooperman views Claude Wheeler as a "war lover" (175) who finds erotic fulfillment only on the battlefield. And James Woodress places *One of Ours* in the tradition of post war disillusionment, another "document of the 'lost generation'" (LL 329).

From this mixed critical heritage, varying perspectives on Cather's friendship theme emerge. Both Woodress and David Stouck liken Claude's friendship with David Gerhardt to the biblical friendship between Jonathan and David. Frederick T. Griffiths finds mythic comparisons with Orpheus and Eurydice, Adam and Eve, and Achilles and Patroclus. In fact, Griffiths claims that of all Cather's novels, *One of Ours* contains "her most overt and extensive use of myth," an achievement that challenges the notion of it as "low-grade, derivative journalism" (263).

The centrality of the Greek model of friendship in *One of Ours* suggests significant features of Cather's classicism. The "value" of *One of Ours* is in the values it upholds. In exploring human experience, Cather revitalizes a Greek ideal, one perhaps best exemplified by the heroism of Achilles and Patroclus. This ideal imbues *One of Ours* with a compelling emotional and symbolic resonance, and it becomes Cather's narrative means to unite the central event in her protagonist's life with his deepest feelings. In Cather the fulfillment of selfhood comes in response to other selves, and it is through masculine friendships forged in war that Claude Wheeler finds meaning in an otherwise meaningless world.

Cather's exploration of male friendship in *One of Ours* follows a time-honored tradition of war literature. Gregory Woods observes that "One of the words most often used in war poetry is 'love'. . . . Sooner or later, in fact, every war seems to have become a time for love, memorable more for its proofs of affection than for those of enmity; and, in particular, a time for young men to love each other" (53). "It follows," he adds, "that the fictional and poetic literature of this time of love, war-time, will have an erotic dimension" (53). Extending this observation, Paul Fussell argues in *The Great War and Modern Memory* that homoeroticism is the imaginative means by which British soldiers remember World War I, and he documents a writing style characterized by "unique physical tenderness, the readiness to admire openly the bodily beauty of young men, [and] the unapologetic recognition that men may be in love with each other" (279–80). Fussell traces this imaginative conception of wartime to factors as diverse as the "need for affection in a largely womanless world" (272), the aesthetic movement's "rediscovery of the erotic attractiveness of young men" (281), and the prewar tradition of homoerotic poetry from Whitman to Hopkins to Housman (282). The enormous popularity of *A Shropshire Lad*, Fussell suggests, "licensed" (282) homoeroticism and directly influenced the stylistic tendency to homoeroticize World War I. In *One of Ours* Cather allies her treatment of male friendship to this literary tradition, and in an unexpected way, homoeroticism authenticates her representation of war as tellingly as direct experience authorizes those of Hemingway and his male contemporaries.[3]

Cather strengthens her homoerotic treatment of war with classical analogues. In *My Ántonia* Jim Burden remembers that his classics professor possessed the ability to recreate "the drama of antique life" (295), and in *One of Ours* Cather again reenvisions a classical culture to develop Claude Wheeler's odyssey toward self-fulfillment. Just as Cather "felt the need for faith" (Woodress, LA 197) during the writing of *One of Ours*, so too does her main character need something to believe in. Vulgar materialism, a devastating world war, empty evangelism, vanished frontiers, and diminished ideals not only threatened the values Cather held in high esteem but underscored the urgent need for something that would redeem a fragmented world and save a dispirited boy.[4] Turning to the ancient world, Cather finds a redemptive ideal in platonic love attainable in ennobling and romantic friendships. Throughout *One of Ours* scattered names like Anchises and Troilus together with Homeric images evoke a classical grandeur. At one point Claude even refers to himself as the hero of the *Odyssey* returning home, supporting the opinion that the events and personages of the Trojan War displace World War I in the novel (Jacks 294). But more is at work in *One of Ours* than derivative techniques and familiar names. As Cather had heroically etched a plow against the setting sun in *My Ántonia*, she evokes in *One of Ours* the brightness of classical ideals and slowly moves her protagonist toward that salvific light.

The structural division of *One of Ours* seemingly disrupts the unity of Cather's method and caused early readers like H. L. Mencken and Sinclair Lewis to praise the Nebraska section while ridiculing the war chapters (see Schroeter 10 and 32). But Cather's narrative strategy is one of tension and resolution, a strategy reinforced by the novel's split design: frustration, anger, and disappointment oppose longing and desire, and in the early books of *One of Ours* realism vigorously thwarts idealism. Claude Wheeler is an intensely idealistic young man and has been since he was a boy. Idealism seems to be part of his nature, something he was born with like his red hair and his love of order. Emphasizing this trait, the novel begins on a note of bright expectancy, sunrise on Lovely Creek, the glorious promise of a splendid day. Yet that promise quickly fades as disorder soon clouds Claude's optimism, and the distasteful chore of carrying animal hides into town spoils his carefree morning.

This initial chapter with its bright beginnings and dashed hopes sets the predominant tone and pattern for the first part of *One of Ours*. Throughout these early chapters, Claude's anxiety directs the narrative tension. He feels himself at odds with most everything and everyone around him. Recurring images of imprisonment reflect this painful psychology as walled cities, captured animals, spiritually confined "children of the moon" (179), an inordinate fear of death, even his own marriage reinforce his despairing mood.

To convey this duality, Cather draws on homosexual literary traditions. Although scenes begin with a Whitmanesque enthusiasm, they end in Housman-like despair; as Lovely Creek resembles the Shropshire countryside, so too does Claude recall Housman's "luckless lads" (*Shropshire Lad* 96). At the Frankfort circus Claude meets his closest friend, Ernest Havel, and together they spend a quiet afternoon outside of town: "The horses stood with their heads over the wagon-box, munching their oats. The stream trick-led by under the willow roots with a cool, persuasive sound. Claude and Ernest lay in the shade, their coats under their heads, talking very little. Occasionally a motor dashed along the road toward town, and a cloud of dust and a smell of gasoline blew in over the creek bottom; but for the most part the silence of the warm, lazy summer noon was undisturbed" (*One of Ours* 12). Their repose is reminiscent of Whitman's enticing "Loafe with me on the grass" in *Song of Myself* (LG 33), but Claude is not usually so at ease with Er-nest; he has always been afraid of being fooled, and his Bohemian friend's carefree speech and relaxed thinking perplex him because he does not yet know himself well enough to fully understand those around him. Moreover, their friendship has always been strained by Claude's relationship with Enid Royce. While others see Ernest and Claude together as natural, they see Claude's mar-riage to Enid as the "wrongest thing in the world" (*One of Ours* 165). Scenes and thoughts of Ernest alternate with scenes and thoughts of Enid. Claude's visits to his Lincoln friends continue this structural pattern. Conversation at the Erlichs' is exciting and spontaneous, whereas "awkwardness" and a "poisonous reticence" (38) inhibit his own family gatherings, and Cather's shifting be-tween Claude's Lincoln visits and his trips home dramatizes his restlessness.

Although socially awkward, alone Claude relaxes in his pine woods or on the unfinished balcony of his house or by bathing in his horse tank. Here too Cather uses subtle sexual imagery to con-vey Claude's feelings, such as the eroticism of the bathing scene. Scenes of boys bathing, simultaneously chaste and erotic, are a fa-miliar aspect of homosexual art and literature, and Cather modifies it throughout her fiction to accommodate her artistic aims; here her aim is autoerotic. Cather surely was familiar with masturbatory passages in literature, if from Whitman if nowhere else:

> The young man that wakes deep at night, the hot hand seeking to
> repress what would master him,

The mystic amorous night, the strange half-welcome pangs,
visions, sweats,
The pulse pounding through palms and trembling encircling
fingers, the young man all color'd, red, ashamed, angry.
("Spontaneous Me," LG 104–05)

Autoerotic imagery also has a precedent in Cather's own fiction. While writing *One of Ours*, Cather wrote "Coming, Aphrodite!" first published in *Smart Set* in August 1920 and later republished in *Youth and the Bright Medusa* (1920). Woodress feels that in "Coming, Aphrodite!" Cather's description of Don Hedger admiring Eden Bower's naked body through a hole in his closet—his "fingers curv[ing] as if he were holding a crayon" (YBM 17) as he imaginatively draws her figure—is "one of the most remarkable scenes Cather ever wrote." Woodress adds, however, that Cather's original editor "would have been startled to have a present-day reader point out to him that the explosive and gesture imagery suggests masturbation" (LL 313–14).

While masturbation in *One of Ours* may indicate Claude's loneliness, it may also represent an assertion of autonomy. At the turn of the century, masturbation would have been another activity prohibited by social and religious discourse and moral reformers like Enid Royce and Brother Weldon. Addressing Whitman's poetic indulgence, Martin argues that "Whitman converts the fear of masturbation into pride, insisting that all his work be interpreted in the light of his 'shameful' sexuality. In an age when masturbation was believed to lead to insanity and the punishment for masturbation was castration, it was an act of considerable courage to write of art through the metaphor of masturbation as often as Whitman did" (HT 72).[5] Similarly, Cather's metaphor seems particularly relevant to her social critique, for masturbation and homosexuality are linked in their challenge of patriarchy. While Enid's refusal of conjugal "rights" rejects patriarchal assumptions, Claude's sexual reverie defies the prohibitive values of the dominant culture that condemn nonprocreative sexual behavior.[6]

Cather introduces erotic possibilities in the early chapters of book 3. Although Leonard Dawson has just left Claude's house, his masculine vitality dominates the scene and transforms the setting into a sexual landscape. While Leonard is happily married and home with his wife, Claude is unhappy and home alone. On his way to his bath, he admires his healthy gourd vine, "feeling grateful to a thing that did so lustily what it was put there to do," and he extends the same feeling to his "well-disposed cow." Reaching the horse tank, Claude undresses and lowers himself inside, lying languidly upon his back. As erotic images float on "invisible currents," Claude's hand makes the only movement in the warm and shadowy water. Rank backyard vines become "Babylon and the hanging gardens," and the "rough" and "prickly" summer squash turn into a sensuously submissive water lily. Eroticism and mysticism unite in a revelatory, explosive moment that "flooded the boy's heart like a second moonrise, flowed through him indefinite and strong, while he lay deathly still for fear of losing it" (177–79).

Cather's masturbatory imagery both frees and restrains, briefly liberating Claude but returning him to guilty thoughts and imprisoning despair. Although the situation resembles Claude's erotic fantasy of being caught naked by Enid, he feels only shame and embarrassment when she returns. Mentioning Leonard Dawson once again, Cather ends the chapter by implicitly contrasting Leonard's happiness with Claude's "unappeased longings and futile dreams" (179). As yet in his life, no transcendent experience saves Claude—his friendship with Ernest becomes tiresome, his visits to the Erlichs' end, and his marriage to Enid, rather than restoring his soul, only increases his loneliness.

Beneath this pervasive tension, Cather's Greek echoes define Claude's dilemma and increasingly offer resolution. The Erlichs' home provides significant revelations for Claude and likewise introduces Cather's alliance with a classical conception of love and friendship. Claude is forewarned by Julius Erlich that "We're all boys at home" (35), and the setting of his first visit emphasizes this masculine exuberance: "The room was full of boys and young men, seated on long divans or perched on the arms of easy chairs, and they were all talking at once. On one of the couches a young man in a smoking jacket lay reading as composedly as if he were alone" (36). Unlike the situation at Claude's own home, where they too are all boys, here Cather evokes the world of Plato's *Symposium*, one of history's most famous texts where an assembly of men and one woman are engaged in lively discourse about love and friendship.[7] With its philosophical inquiry, its theories of idealized love, and its dialectic patterns of discovery, the *Symposium* provides a touchstone to the provocative classicism of Cather's novel. Upon entering the Erlichs' home, Claude intuits a platonic vitality, "the sense of being in a warm and gracious atmosphere, charged with generous enthusiasms and ennobled by romantic friendships" (73).

Although Claude experiences a "happy unconsciousness" (39) at the Erlichs', back home his soul remains a languishing captive, intensified by the renewed "conviction that there was something splendid about life, if he could but find it!" (90). To dramatize Claude's anguish Cather once again alludes to Plato, this time his *Phaedrus*, in which the human soul is likened to a charioteer and two winged horses. Immediately after Claude's mental struggle between something splendid and sordid reality, Cather places him in a sleigh managing "two wiry little blacks, Pompey and Satan" (91). Cather's team is metaphorically linked to Plato's horses, the sleigh to his chariot, and Claude to its charioteer. The ride itself is analogous to a journey toward spiritual freedom.

Cather's horse imagery and its relationship to a classical myth is particularly suggestive in *One of Ours*. Bernice Slote writes that "Like any writer who uses myth organically, Willa Cather had some habitual emotional values for particular stories or figures, and by the invocation of a name could gather in the whole body of associations" ("First Principles" 97). Cather's reference to Euripides' *Hippolyta* offers one clue to the origin of her horse imagery; Claude's frequent association with animals evokes other classical possibilities. Early in the novel he contends with two balking mules, and later an unruly team drags him into a barbed wire fence.

Like classical heroes, Claude often reveals affection for a favorite horse, and his meditative bathing in the horse tank broadens this allusive scheme. Claude himself is at times "unyielding," and at one point he is metaphorically harnessed "as if he had a bridle-bit in his mouth" (48). Slote points out that a young Cather once viewed the soul as a musical instrument, indicated by an passage in a book among Cather's possessions that read "The soul . . . may be compared to a stringed instrument" (*April Twilights* xxxvii). In *One of Ours* Cather adopts a more complex metaphor to reveal the complexities of her protagonist, borrowing for her story Plato's view of the soul as a struggling charioteer.

Cather strengthens her Greek parallels early in the novel by uniting the twin themes of freedom and heroic idealism. Upon entering the Erlichs' lively home, Claude enters a world of new possibilities. In a room filled with agreeable people, vibrant conversation, and interesting objects, a bust of Byron captures Claude's attention and "for some reason instantly made him wish he lived there" (37). In a later scene Julius Erlich insists that Claude immediately read a biography of Garibaldi. These two freedom fighters—Byron for Greek independence and Garibaldi for a unified Italy—symbolically point to the heroes of antiquity; fighting for freedom is itself a classical tradition, often linked with friendship and martyrdom. Such associations draw attention to Claude's unrest and his own struggle for independence. The familiar image of Claude is a Byronic one, lost in forlorn thought or brooding beside his windmill, wondering what was the matter with him. Byron and Garibaldi offer moral alternatives to Claude: he can either languish at home, forever a captive, or find liberation in a heroic cause. With the increased fighting in Europe, suddenly Paris "had come to have the purity of an abstract idea" (149). The most redemptive act for Claude is to join the American Expeditionary Force, and the fight to save France becomes as well a fight for personal salvation.

Claude's transformation begins when he enters the army. Here too Cather dramatically shifts her narrative focus from the destiny of France to her emerging friendship theme and, in doing so, begins to strengthen affinities with homosexual myth and gay literary traditions. In a passage of vibrant cataloguing again recalling Whitman, Cather describes Claude's compassion for the men in his unit:

> They had come together from farms and shops and mills and mines, boys from college and boys from tough joints in big cities; sheepherders, street car drivers, plumbers' assistants, billiard markers. Claude had seen hundreds of them when they first came in; "show men" in cheap, loud sport suits, ranch boys in knitted waistcoats, machinists with the grease still on their fingers, farm-hands like Dan, in their one Sunday coat. Some of them carried paper suitcases tied up with rope, some brought all they had in a blue handkerchief. But they all came to give and not to ask, and what they offered was just themselves; their big red hands, their strong backs, the steady, honest, modest look in their eyes. (213)

In addition to its Whitmanesque style, the masculine vitality of Cather's catalog also hints at her homoeroticism, implying what Fussell describes as the erotic appeal of soldiers in general, "their youth, their athleticism, their relative cleanliness, their uniforms, and their heroic readiness, like Adonis or St. Sebastian, for 'sacrifice'" (278).[8] Following this exuberant tallying, Cather adds that "Claude loved the men he trained with,—wouldn't choose to live in any better company" (214), an idea further evoking Whitman's "threads of manly friendships" ("Democratic Vistas," CP 493).

On his way home after basic training, Claude muses on his sense of freedom and discovery: "how this country that had once seemed little and dull to him, now seemed large and rich in variety. During the months in camp he had been wholly absorbed in new work and new friendships, and now his own neighbourhood came to him with the freshness of things that have been forgotten for a long while,—came together before his eyes as a harmonious whole. He was going away, and he would carry the whole countryside in his mind, meaning more to him than it ever had before" (218–19). Claude's conversion, his "coming home," begins after his having known the companionship of other men and learned the value of their friendship. This redemptive experience emotionally defines his new sense of self, an identity quite unlike his earlier perception of the "prosaic and commonplace" (111) world of men. His "going away" continues Cather's homosexual imagery, for "going away" is often a gay motif, found for example in the travel literature of Charles Warren Stoddard or the sea fiction of Herman Melville.[9] Cather's "voyage" metaphor—announced by the section title "Voyage on the *Anchises*"—underscores her emerging theme of personal growth. In this sense Claude's going away is doubly suggestive, for he is going both to "another country" in general and to France in particular, Cather's symbol of erotic freedom.[10] As Margaret Cruikshank writes in *The Gay and Lesbian Liberation Movement*, "When the hero of Willa Cather's novel *One of Ours* goes to France to fight in World War I, he discovers an exciting new world of variety, expansiveness, and emotion which he had never dreamed of while living as a farmer. He becomes deeply dissatisfied with his former life, including his marriage" (29).

As Claude begins to make himself over, so too does Cather revise the pattern of her story from a narrative strategy emphasizing tension to one stressing resolution. Classical imagery reconciles the dichotomy between a Whitmanesque exuberance and a Housman-like despair. The "Wooden ships" (230) at the dockyards, like the famed Trojan Horse, anticipate Cather's intensified use of Greek myth and classical allusion to further develop her theme of redeeming friendship, while the transition aboard the troopship *Anchises* announces Claude's heroic odyssey by placing him in a lineage of Greek wanderer-warriors, himself the progenitor of heroic ideals.

Ironically, the farther Claude travels toward war, the closer he arrives at peace. Although glorious weather gives way to threatening skies and an attack of influenza turns the *Anchises* into a death ship, Claude's idealism remains undaunted. Rather than denying the truth, Claude's behavior reveals another reality, an imaginative process by which an ideal becomes real. During the voyage itself,

Cather's language reflects Claude's personal discoveries amid the destructiveness of war. Words like "splendid," "brave," "noble," and "glorious" appear throughout. Initially satiric, they echo disturbing war propaganda found in literature of the "Great War" and later disparaged by writers of the Hemingway school. Yet such words also recall Claude's comments to Mrs. Erlich after first visiting her home, his complimentary "It's been lovely'" (39). While earlier he had been emotionally tentative, here his language fluently avows the perceptual drama taking shape in his mind, a drama intensified more by the men around him than the war they are destined to fight.

Claude's experiences aboard the *Anchises* reveal how a growing intimacy with his men advances his self-awareness, and Cather's friendship theme unifies them into a reflective pattern of discovery. While nursing his men, Claude recognizes the practical need to wear a wristwatch. As he once would never have entered a saloon, or bought dinner at the Frankfort hotel for fear of his family's censure, or worn a wristwatch because he thought it effeminate, now Claude's experiences alter his self-perception, and likewise those new perceptions affect his behavior. Claude's repose is in part attributable to his escaping confining gender conventions. War provides opportunities for alternatives, and in making himself over, Claude firmly resists the cultural authority forcing him to live through an "aesthetic proxy" (98). Aboard the *Anchises* Claude reasserts the nurturing and caring role he often assumed at home; he admires the captain's neat and comfortable quarters and enjoys visiting him there; and he wears a wristwatch unselfconsciously and without embarrassment.

Another immensely revealing incident in this section of the novel is Claude's interest in the handsome marine Albert Usher. From among so many men, Claude singles out this individual for close observation: "There was on board a solitary Marine, with the stripes of Border service on his coat. He had been sick in the Navy Hospital in Brooklyn when his regiment sailed, and was now going over to join it. He was a young fellow, rather pale from his recent illness, but he was exactly Claude's idea of what a soldier ought to look like. His eye followed the Marine about all day" (240). As Albert stands out from others, so too does he stand out in the novel. Albert represents to Claude all that he himself wants to be and has always thought he was not. Part of Claude's distress has been an agonizing self-persecution, whether for the color of his hair, the shape of his head, or his disagreeable family ties; another part of Claude's dilemma is overcoming his painful self-reproach.[11] His observing Albert Usher resolves that tension. Claude discerns Usher's inner worth from his outer appearance: well-shaped bones and a handsome head reveal moral strength. Other characters in the novel observe similar characteristics in Claude, the very things that he so often condemns in himself. Gladys Farmer, Mrs. Erlich and her cousin, Claude's mother and Mahailey, Mr. Royce, Peachy Millmore, even his brother Bayliss—all admire in Claude what he fails to value: his strong physique, a manly appearance, fine inner traits. Claude, however, takes his physique for granted, seeing instead only a "hayseed" or "chump" (17), and repeatedly hears "Clod" (179) rather than "Claude" from his wife.

Albert and Claude are strikingly alike, a similarity evoking the sexual connotations of "twinship" as argued in the *Symposium* and the erotic ambiguities of "brotherhood."[12] Even their personal histories are similar, for others have also sensed Usher's fine qualities—one man offering to finance his education, an element of male patronage further charging the episode with homoerotic intensity. Claude's staring at Usher reverses the incidents of others staring at him. Again Claude's behavior reveals rebirth, a pattern later verbalized by Victor Morse—another imprisoned individual liberating himself from the "glass cage" (281) of his father's small-town bank—and echoed by Mlle. de Courcy in describing the American soldier as the "new man" (332). By observing Albert, Claude unconsciously discovers a self he can admire.

Claude's relationship with David Gerhardt completes his transformation and reemphasizes the redemptive values Cather finds in friendship and her rendering them through homosexual imagery.

Surpassing what Fussell describes as the "sentimental associations" and "protective affection" (274) of wartime friendships, Claude and David's relationship comes closer to the intensity of the Sacred Band. In meeting David, Claude recognizes something he has been seeking all his life, someone he can admire unfailingly. Indeed, the search for the ideal friend is a recurrent theme in gay literature. Other details of their relationship also follow the pattern of the Greek ideal. Although close in age to Claude, David looks older and more worldly. As he is with Ernest, Claude is at first suspicious, careful not to be fooled, but he gradually relaxes. The pine woods resemble his beloved timber lot in Nebraska, and his walks with David recall those with Ernest along Lovely Creek. In France the trees are like "old Grecian lyres" (300), another detail reinforcing Cather's theme. Their home together is peaceful, a sanctuary in the midst of war, made comfortable by mutual affection rather than material objects like those with which Ralph sets up housekeeping in Colorado. And rather than the comic mismanagement of the two "bachelor" sheep-ranchers who lived on Trevor Hill or the cold arrangement of Enid's kitchen, Claude and David's domestic affairs reflect the settled warmth of French culture.

Claude's redemptive friendship with David Gerhardt amplifies the homoerotic aura of *One of Ours*, and Cather's development of their relationship mirrors her evocation of homosexuality throughout the novel. In particular, Claude and David's sylvan retreats illustrate the novel's "démeublé" process, for when they enter the secluded French woods, Cather enters the world of homosexual pastoral. Drawing upon a literary tradition that runs from Virgil's second eclogue to Whitman's "In Paths Untrodden" and Housman's "land of lost content" (*Shropshire Lad* 57), Cather homoeroticizes her pastoral setting—a setting already eroticized by the French curé's niece and her German lover. Byrne Fone writes that "Those who would dwell in Arcadia seek out that secret Eden because of its isolation from the troubled world and its safety from the arrogant demands of those who would deny freedom, curtail human action, and destroy innocence and love" ("This Other

Eden" 13). Claude and David find that protective space, and in its silence, readers feel the presence of Cather's "thing not named," an emotional aura that evokes gay experience. Incidental details of Claude and David's closeness and enclosure further intimate homosexuality: sleep as an escape from war and entry into the realm of love, the classical benediction of male friendship, a Hellenistic eros flowering within an Arcadian setting, and "rest" as a sexual metaphor.[13] Reversing Claude's loneliness in his woods back home, in France he meets the longed-for friend, and in sublime understatement Cather conveys his transformation: "When they retraced their steps, the wood was full of green twilight. Their relations had changed somewhat during the last half hour, and they strolled in confidential silence up the home-like street to the door of their own garden" (301–02). The redemptive power of friendship relieves Claude's loneliness and restores his soul.

To further signify her theme, Cather continues her characteristic mirroring device, and seemingly familiar scenes assume new meanings. In the French woods David and Claude rest quietly. A young girl slips suddenly upon them and gazes at Claude. Rather than tense and rigid as he had been on the courthouse steps in Denver, struggling with bright uncertainties, Claude is now relaxed, and the French girl sees the beauty of repose rather than the rebellious energy that had impressed the Denver onlooker. There the statue of Kit Carson, symbolically closing the West to heroic endeavor, and Claude's equally statuesque pose sharply defined his distress. Both Cather and Claude seek heroic action elsewhere. In France, Claude discovers a redeeming truth in friendship, and its salutary effect is evident in his repose. Alluding to Plato once again, Cather returns to the charioteer image to emphasize Claude's change. After reconciling the tension in his life, Claude dreams of himself as a boy in Nebraska, "out in the ploughed fields, where he could see nothing but the furrowed brown earth, stretching from horizon to horizon. Up and down it moved a boy, with a plough and two horses" (349). While the earlier sleigh scene heightened Claude's tension, a fretful dream of endless plowing spiritually reawakens him. Even Cather's language mirrors itself to intensify the Greek ideal: Claude's impassioned "something splendid" (48) and philosophic "something else" (357) resound as David's triumphant "something Olympian" (348)—certainly the cumulative resonance throughout *One of Ours* is of "something" homosexual.

Cather's conceptual strengths in *One of Ours* lay in patterns such as these that indirectly recreate an antique drama of love and friendship. As a result, minor scenes often provide us her closest parallels with the ideals of the Sacred Band. For instance, when Claude and his sergeant go behind the lines at dark, they join a group of English soldiers. Not until daylight do they have an opportunity to observe one of their companions, and Cather's description of him glows with meaning: "As it began to grow light, the two Americans wondered more and more at the extremely youthful appearance of their companion. When they stopped at a shellhole and washed the mud from their faces, the English boy, with his helmet off and the weather stains removed, showed a countenance of adolescent freshness, almost girlish; cheeks like pink apples, yellow curls above his forehead, long, soft lashes" (319–20). This brief description encapsulates and encodes the sexual aesthetics of *One of Ours*. While a variation of the male bathing scenes so familiar in homosexual art, it also ignites an explosion of literary echoes, from twentieth-century fiction to the tender lyrics of classical poetry. The English boy incarnates the Greek ideal, existing as both a radiant Apollo and the beautiful Antinous. His modern lineage includes Housman's athletes dying young and Thomas Mann's mesmeric Tadzio, as well as Billy Budd and Dorian Gray.[14]

A homoerotic motif of masculine beauty runs throughout *One of Ours* and is a vital corollary to its friendship theme. While juxtaposing the innocence and vulnerability of youth against the horrors of war, this narrative technique stresses Cather's classical sensibility and her method of bringing it to fictional life. Explaining Plato's "ladder of love," Bullough writes that "the object of love, in

Plato's terms, was to procreate and beget the sphere of the 'beauti-ful'" (109) and that "love represented an aspiration toward a higher perfection, an ideal of excellence" (108). For the Greeks, physical beauty manifested a spiritual continuum toward an aesthetic ideal, and as Bullough reminds us, "The Greek idea of beauty was, of course, masculine rather than feminine" (100). In particular, male adolescence in the form of the Greek ephebe epitomizes classical standards of beauty. Fair-haired and blue-eyed, Claude possesses the physical attributes of the Greek ideal and slowly attains its spir-itual illumination. Adapting this philosophy in *One of Ours,* Cather evokes a crucial platonic paradigm: the unseen is made visible, and abstract Beauty is realized by its physical correlative.

Cather continues her Greek allusions with the young soldier's explanation of the "Pal Batallion" (320), a large unit of school friends who enlisted in the war together and whose survivors now number only seventeen, including him. This modern rendition of the Sacred Band closely approximates the ideals of the ancient army of lovers, where a young man fought bravely at the side of an older protector in a formal procedure sanctioned by social and mil-itary codes. All three hundred members of the Sacred Band were killed at Chaeronea in 338 BC but displayed such remarkable valor that the victorious Philip, father of Alexander the Great, commem-orated their exceptional efforts.[15] While Griffiths sees the English boy's story as the novel's "supreme example of courage" (274), other possibilities combine with this interpretation to enlarge its purpose. Beauty, loyalty, youth, and courage coalesce in this one character, afterward broadening into a more inclusive pattern.

The Swedish band boys aboard the *Anchises* share this Hellenic dedication and promulgate the ideals of the Sacred Band: "They were the town band, had enlisted in a body, had gone into training together, and had never been separated. . . . They hung together in a quiet, determined way, and if you began to talk to one, you soon found that all the others were there" (236). Reference to their hometown newspaper, the *Hillport Argus,* alerts readers to their symbolic origins as once again a single word or phrase summons a whole body of association. Their distinction, like that of the Greek warrior-lovers, is in their uncommon loyalty and sacrifice. Pairs of men—Hicks and Able, Louis and Emile, and of course Claude and David—also participate in Cather's mythologizing pattern and implicitly strengthen her Achilles and Patroclus analogy. Even individuals—like the English boy-soldier and the young violinist Lucien—display an inspiring Hellenic ardor. In addition, Cather describes other heroic attachments among the soldiers that embody the Greek ideal. Two men plan to open a garage after the war, and when one is killed, the other decides to name the garage after the two of them in tribute to his fallen companion. The men also notice photographs nailed upon crosses marking soldiers' graves, "left by some comrade to perpetuate his memory a little longer" (335).

Seeing the novel this way prepares a reader for the German sniper scene and charges that remarkably curious episode with new meaning. As Woodress points out, the story was told to Cather by an American officer, and she so liked his naïveté that she included it in *One of Ours* to show Claude's innocence (LL 332–33). While this explanation provides insight into Cather's source, it overlooks the imaginative impact the anecdote makes upon a reader and its contribution to Cather's narrative strategy.

I would argue that Cather used the story for its ambiguity as well as its explicitness. The idea of a delicate silver locket around a German officer's neck, carrying the likeness of "a young man, pale as snow, with blurred forget-me-not eyes" (367), surely surprises a reader as much as it does Cather's soldiers and challenges expectations all around. Foremost, it challenges gender expectations as a man is wearing it rather than a woman, as occurs in conventional locket-related stories. In addition, the scene upsets expectations inherent in the novel itself as Cather here modifies the earlier episode where Claude examines the effects of one of his casualties at sea. And the picture of a young man, "a poet, or something" rather than a "beautiful woman" (367) provokes an even wider challenge. While David is "disdainful" (367), Claude is curious and compassionate, a further example of his increasing inquiry into things, of his making himself over.

Admiring Cather's forthrightness in introducing homosexuality into her story, Woodress adds that the scene "makes clear" that David and Claude's relationship is "purely platonic" (LL 333). I would go further than this and suggest that rather than simply introducing homosexuality into her story, the scene underscores male love as the major theme of *One of Ours*. But while the episode may indicate that Claude and David's relationship is platonic, it is unlikely that that fact is meant as pejorative of homosexuality; rather, Cather's German officer is an ambiguously emblematic character, both "one of ours" in his homosexuality and "Other" in his demonization, a position not unlike the one in which some of Claude's German-American neighbors find themselves back home. While Griffiths sees the scene as a perversion of the Greek ideal, a chilling example of "Teutonic decadence" (266) and "subhuman viciousness" (267), Robert Nelson views David's disdain as a reaction to Claude rather than to the officer and his male lover, and "in telling Bert to leave [the locket] on the body, he is respecting that relationship" (39).[16]

As different as they are, these interpretations all evoke the tradition to which Cather repeatedly alludes throughout *One of Ours*—platonic love and the Greek ideal. As Plato distinguishes between spiritual, idealized love and sensual desire and provides a model for transcendence, so too does Cather esteem emotional intimacy without sexuality. This is the Greek ideal that saves Claude. The German officer and his young lover join the other male pairs in providing Claude with new understanding of himself and his relationship with David, and they reveal to the reader how the ideals of the Sacred Band intricately shape that knowledge.

Although Cather's sexual aesthetics implicitly endorse Claude's spiritual growth, the notion of that growth has been challenged by scholars. Critical emphasis on Claude as a "blockhead" and "buffoon" reduce his emotional complexity to caricature, and Cather's own statement about her hero "not see[ing] pictures" (quoted in

Bohlke 39) erects formidable interpretative barriers. Cather's admission of a hidden Parsifal theme also diverts attention from other possibilities.[17]

A gay reading of *One of Ours* reinvigorates its allegorical value, an interpretation supported by Griffith's sense of Claude as Cather's "héros démeublé" (270). Claude may be "an inarticulate young man butting his way through the world" (quoted in Bohlke 78), as Cather described her protagonist, but the delicacy of his feelings heroizes him. Gladys Farmer's esteem for Claude further evokes his personal heroism as she sympathetically associates him with others in Frankfort "who had imagination and generous impulses" (135). Tellingly, Claude's affinities with Bobbie Jones, "the effeminate drug clerk" (135), place him in direct literary kinship with Erik Valborg in Sinclair Lewis's *Main Street* (1920) and Wing Biddlebaum in Sherwood Anderson's short story "Hands" (1919), two of American literature's most famous homosexual characters.

This view of Claude strengthens the unity of the novel. With David resting at his side, Claude conceives that "Life was so short that it meant nothing at all unless it were continually reinforced by something that endured; unless the shadows of individual existence came and went against a background that held together" (345). Here Cather's "something" is remarkably close to Whitman's "adhesiveness," and for Claude, as for Cather, friendship provides that cohering fabric.[18] In creating "something that endured," Cather fuses the immortality of a classical style with the immutability of classical ideals. Rosowski writes that at the end of *One of Ours*, "comradeship is the reality, the war strangely unreal. Even in battle, when his company is defending the Boar's Snout and Claude leaps to the parapet to encourage his men, he is oblivious to the violence around him, thinking only that he commanded wonderful men and that David would find them all there when he returned: these are the ideals of devotion, fidelity, trust, and, most importantly, love" (VP 112). This too is the Greek ideal, the heroic banner of the Sacred Band; and Claude's final thoughts of "mortal" but "unconquerable" (386) intuit its spiritual truth.

Yet questions still emerge from this ending. Is Claude's final re-alization another ideal that would have been shattered by postwar disillusionment? Would Claude have been another soul trapped in the "lost generation"? Is Cather indicting heroic idealism or unin-spired reality? Finally, is *One of Ours* her satire or her literal truth? I think that while Cather wishes readers to reject false ideals, she wants them at the same time to consider the view that abstract ideas can be sources of enormous power. Her shifting the story from a war that broke the world in two to the friendship that held it together realizes that desire.

Throughout the novel, narrative hints move us in this direction. Although an interplay of dark and light continues throughout the story, Claude's life ends at sunrise—the time of day when he makes his personal discoveries and when Cather's story of his life begins. Narrative tension is quietly relaxed. As images of imprisonment in-form Claude's early life, his death integrates patterns of freedom and release. Bright beginnings, "The Star-Spangled Banner," Ma-hailey's "Blazing Star" quilt, saved especially for Claude, emotion-ally reappear and surround Claude with a saintly radiance. Claude's self-discoveries during the war symbolically distinguish him from the "Soldat Inconnu" (335) who also died for France, and after his death, his story lovingly continues, like those of the ancient heroes that it resembles. And Cather's "delicately rendered deification" (Rosowski, "Subverted Endings" 80) at the very end of the novel doubly affirms heroic possibilities: "Mrs. Wheeler always feels that God is near,—but Mahailey is not troubled by any knowledge of interstellar spaces, and for her He is nearer still,—directly over-head, not so very far above the kitchen stove" (391). Here Chris-tian traditions blend with classical allusion; as Emperor Hadrian deified Antinous to perpetuate his memory, Cather likewise deifies Claude to affirm his life.

Friendship, not war, is the regenerative force sanctioned throughout *One of Ours*, and it creates the spiritual and imaginative unity felt at the novel's close. Rather than "a troublingly nihilistic text" (Gelfant 97), *One of Ours* is perhaps Cather's most affirmative novel. Recognizing Cather's high regard for male friendship, Erik Ingvar Thurin wonders why she chose "this strange way of honoring the average American doughboy" (246). Cather selected one of literature's most enduring traditions, that of Greek love, to tell Claude's story. Through the redeeming value of friendship, the book comes together as a whole, as does Claude himself. Cather's Sacred Band echoes the classical origins of this ideal and allows Claude to discover the "holy thoughts" (111) he once felt belonged only to women.

As it does in Whitman, male friendship also registers Cather's social critique, for the material wasteland of America is here offset by the spiritualization of what Whitman calls "manly love" ("For You O Democracy," LG 117).[19] For Whitman, the possibilities of friendship could unify the nation; for Cather, male friendship is a symbol for psychic wholeness. This treatment of friendship further marks *One of Ours* as a "turning point" (Woodress, LL 334) in Cather's canon as it anticipates her later narrative directions—in *The Professor's House* Cather implicitly includes friendship among the sources of human happiness, and in *Death Comes for the Archbishop* she continues to explore its value, for in fusing friendship, art, and religion, Father Latour's long life serenely realizes the heroic vision Claude momentarily glimpsed the morning of his death.

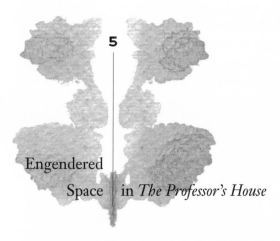

5

Engendered
Space in *The Professor's House*

SEXUAL aesthetics in *The Professor's House* (1925)
continue to link homosexuality with spiritual experience, but while
the novel is as homoerotic as *One of Ours*, its narrative strategy is
significantly different. Susan J. Rosowski comments that "Cather
abandoned the search of her previous characters for value outside
themselves and set Godfrey St. Peter on an internal quest for that
which is real, through public roles to an original identity" (VP 131).
In a novel richly informed by structural analogies, homosexuality
emerges as Cather's most potent metaphor for this redemptive
quest.

Doris Grumbach poses the perennial question about *The Professor's House*: "what is wrong with the professor?" ("A Study" 336).
Given few textual clues, critics attempt plausible explanations. For
example, Rosowski writes that "St. Peter is the first of what was to
be a gallery of Cather's characters to confront the modern threat of
annihilation" (VP 136), Merrill Maguire Skaggs describes the professor as "immensely complex and tired" (185), and Leon Edel argues that St. Peter "grieves not for a lost love; he is simply alien-
ated" ("A Cave" 214). Grumbach provocatively answers her own
question: "For it seems clear to me that the professor's problem lies

in his late and blinding realization that the life he had been leading, the life of father and husband, is, and always has been, a false one for him, that his existence within these roles is no longer bearable, and that death is preferable to living any longer in the stifling, elaborately furnished, and *false* (for him) house of women and marriage" ("A Study" 337). Cather's treatment of homosexuality in *The Professor's House* extends these interpretations and provides an indirect clue to understanding her profoundly depressed professor.

If Cather's extreme evasiveness makes *The Professor's House* her "most experimental" novel (Stout 87), then homosexuality is its most appropriate signifier. Glen Love writes that "The movement toward modernism in fiction was, of course, marked by an emergence, from many sources, of private languages, symbolist resonances, intuitive communications, all of which serve to foreground style, and many of which involved understatement and indirection" (306). Cather's theory of the "unfurnished novel" anticipates the modernist movement in literary history; more specifically, her sexual aesthetics anticipate contemporary theories about homosexuality. In *Homosexuality: The Psychology of the Creative Process* Paul Rosenfels argues that "It is the homosexual above all others who is in a position to search for an inner identity in the civilized world" (140), and the novelist John Rechy asserts that "The homosexual is the clearest symbol of alienation and despair. And nobility" (quoted in Stephen Adams 96). *The Professor's House* explores this diversity, immobilizing St. Peter between happiness and despair. Cather's characteristic technique reinforces her theme as the ambiguous "something" recurs in the narrative with palpable intensity. The "something splendid" Claude Wheeler finds before his death is akin to the "something very precious" Godfrey St. Peter relinquishes in order to go on living. Both works affirm male friendship, but while the earlier novel celebrates its discovery, *The Professor's House* laments its loss.

In casting St. Peter's love for Tom Outland as that between a teacher and his student, Cather follows in a tradition of homoerotic literature ranging from the "pedagogic eros of the Greeks"

(Crompton 268) to Henry James's "The Pupil" (1890). Pupil and master relationships also have a long foreground in her own fiction. For instance, in "The Professor's Commencement" (1902) the tender affection of Professor Graves for his "pupil with the gentle eyes and manner of a girl" (CSF 290) haunts Cather's early story; the relationship between Harvey Merrick and Henry Steavens in "The Sculptor's Funeral" creates a lingering emotional resonance; and the mutual admiration between Lucius Wilson and Alexander Bartley in *Alexander's Bridge* (1912) fosters an enduring friendship between the professor and his former student. And just as Gaston Cleric's ability to recreate antique life in *My Ántonia* looks forward to the classicism of *One of Ours*, so his friendship with Jim Burden anticipates the emotional center of *The Professor's House*.

Unlike these other relationships, the friendship between Professor St. Peter and Tom Outland is more overtly eroticized. Cather significantly suffuses descriptions of her central characters with their physical appeal. From the beginning of the novel, St. Peter is defined by physical attractiveness, from his "very black hair" (13) to his impressive physique: "The Professor in pyjamas was not an unpleasant sight; for looks, the fewer clothes he had on, the better. Anything that clung to his body showed it to be built upon extremely good bones, with the slender hips and springy shoulders of a tireless swimmer" (12). Upon first meeting Tom Outland, St. Peter responds to the younger man's physical appearance. Collecting impressions such as Tom's "manly, mature voice" and his suntanned face and fair forehead, St. Peter concludes approvingly: "The boy was fine-looking, he saw—tall and presumably well built" (112). Cather intensifies the professor's reaction by centering it upon Tom's outstretched hand, a focus blending his physical observations with an emerging emotional response: "'Hold them still a moment,' said the Professor, looking down, not at the turquoises, but at the hand that held them: the muscular, many-lined palm, the long, strong fingers with soft ends, the straight little finger, the flexible, beautifully shaped thumb that curved back from the rest of the hand as if it were its own master. What a hand! He could see it yet, with the blue stones lying in it" (121).

Tom is not like the other college boys, and Cather emphasizes his difference through physical details, as he "Always had something in his voice, in his eyes" (132). This uniqueness transforms Tom's physical reality into a "glittering" (111) and often "fugitive" (132) idea, an abstraction encompassing the erotically ambiguous relationships of brother, son, pupil, and friend. The erotic nature of Tom's and the professor's physical descriptions is also heightened by contrast with the "painfully unattractive" (50) Professor Crane. And the intimacy of their scenes together further evokes the homoeroticism of Cather's text, a physical and emotional closeness prompting Lillian St. Peter's fierce jealousy and increasing coldness "after the Professor began to take Tom up to the study and talk over his work with him, began to make a companion of him" (173). As Grumbach writes, "St. Peter's deepest feelings are invoked when he first meets Tom. . . . This admiration strikes us as somewhat excessive until we begin to understand that the professor's inhibited heart is beginning to be filled by Tom" ("A Study" 339). Sexual aesthetics portray this change of heart: Tom's hand is the focus of the professor's desiring gaze; Tom himself is the object of his emotional desire.

Great friendship in *The Professor's House* is Cather's compelling theme, and her treatment of it enhances the novel's "extraordinary suggestiveness" (Grumbach, "A Study" 337). Depicting male friendship, Cather also delineates her narrative method. In *One of Ours* Cather adopts a classical ideal of friendship and leads Claude toward its salvation. Increasingly threatened by a world torn apart, Cather enlarges her scope in *The Professor's House* to include other redemptive models. Classical ideals alone no longer suffice amid rampant materialism, personal loss, and spiritual decline—a time Rosowski describes as "that historical moment when things broke apart: science from religion, thought from feeling, the present from the past" (VP 135). Seeking ways to redeem her world, Cather explores other possibilities for renewal. Mary Ruth Ryder observes that "*The Professor's House* begins more explicitly to develop Cather's dialectic between the imagery from classical myth and allusions to Christian myth" (220). To strengthen this dialectic, Cather shifts the emphasis of her Sacred Band from its military power to its spiritual force. As he reflects upon Tom's upbringing and early associations, the professor's notion of love among the working men illustrates Cather's inclusive technique: "There is, he knew, this dream of self-sacrificing friendship and disinterested love down among the day-labourers, the men who run the railroad trains and boats and reapers and thrashers and mine-drills of the world" (172). Blending Christian and classical patterns of friendship with a distinctly Whitmanesque exuberance, Cather combines the heroism of the Sacred Band with Christian benevolence and self-sacrifice.[1]

Structural analogies also hint at homosexuality in Cather's design. Her commentary on *The Professor's House* identifies "two experiments in form" which she attempted in her writing: the inset story and the musical sonata (see "On *The Professor's House*" 30–31). Centering "Tom Outland's Story" within her narrative, Cather inserts the "nouvelle" into the "roman" while the three movements of a sonata—"despairing," "rhapsodical," and "muted" (Edward and Lillian Bloom 161)—parallel the three sections of the novel. By evoking "the thing not named," the erotic aura of Tom Outland's "unusual background" (PH 132) and his emotional impact upon St. Peter underscore Cather's explorations in form.

The novel begins with the professor's despair. Although "The moving was over and done" (11), St. Peter remains in his old study; memories of Tom Outland make him reluctant to move into his new house. Tom affects the professor like his story affects the narrative: both are simultaneously disruptive and liberating. Again physical details register this feeling. St. Peter's eyes reflect his disposition as the novel begins: "They had lost none of their fire, though just now the man behind them was feeling a diminution of ardour" (13). Toward the end of the novel, he recalls that "Just when the morning brightness of the world was wearing off for him, along came Outland and brought him a kind of second youth"

(258). Alternating between moods of despair and delight, the novel ends, as does a sonata, with the muting of feeling.

Sexual aesthetics foreground this stifling of emotional expression. Tom's relationship with Roddy Blake, "the remarkable friend" (123), is—like St. Peter's relationship with Tom—characterized by deep, often conflicted feelings of desire and restraint. This tension is most strongly expressed by Tom's inability to keep Roddy from leaving the Blue Mesa even though in his heart he wished him to stay: "There was an ache in my arms to reach out and detain him, but there was something else that made me absolutely powerless to do so" (247). The professor's own emotional reserve parallels Tom's. Such restraint evokes the muting of a sonata, and as a result, as Janis Stout observes, "the stifling of emotional expression, the impossibility of understanding or being understood, occupies the center of the novel" (89).

In contrast to these formal experiments, Cather describes a third compositional metaphor shaping *The Professor's House:*

> Just before I began the book I had seen, in Paris, an exhibition of old and modern Dutch paintings. In many of them the scene presented was a living-room warmly furnished, or a kitchen full of food and coppers. But in most of the interiors, whether drawing-room or kitchen, there was a square window, open, through which one saw the masts of ships, or a stretch of grey sea. The feeling of the sea that one got through those square windows was remarkable, and gave me a sense of the fleets of Dutch ships that ply quietly on all the waters of the globe—to Java, etc. ("On *The Professor's House*" 31)

The variety and abundance of Cather's sources suggest her experimentalism in *The Professor's House* and justify the "structural audacity" (Love 300) of Tom Outland's story. Their sexual suggestions provide another narrative link and further intensify Cather's technical and thematic complexity.

Spatial metaphors such as houses and rooms, towers and caves, doors and windows dominate *The Professor's House* and create tension in the novel through the poetics of engendered space. Cather draws attention to this artistic strategy as she elaborates upon her narrative method: "In my book I tried to make Professor St. Peter's house rather overcrowded and stuffy with new things; American proprieties, clothes, furs, petty ambitions, quivering jealousies— until one got rather stifled. Then I wanted to open the square window and let in the fresh air that blew off the Blue Mesa, and the fine disregard of trivialities which was in Tom Outland's face and in his behaviour" ("On *The Professor's House*" 31–32). To escape stifling space, Cather evokes male friendship, and when she metaphorically opens a window, the view is very often homoerotic. Throughout *The Professor's House* imaginative, redemptive space— that which is out there, through the open window, elsewhere rather than here—is erotically engendered.[2]

In addition to her formal analogies, Cather implicitly compares her narrative to "a turquoise set in dull silver" (PH 107). Within the context of *The Professor's House* the color blue becomes not only symbolic of spirituality but emblematic as well of the spiritualization of male friendship.[3] Opening his study window, the professor sees the blue of Lake Michigan: "But the great fact in life, the always possible escape from dullness, was the lake. The sun rose out of it, the day began there; it was like an open door that nobody could shut. The land and all its dreariness could never close in on you. You had only to look at the lake, and you knew you would soon be free" (30). For St. Peter, the lake symbolizes freedom, its setting physically and spiritually liberating, its blue "quite another blue" (31). His male company there provides an escape from marriage and the world of women. All-male companionship runs throughout Cather's fiction such as the recurring image of a group of boys around a campfire, teachers and pupils, and adult friends. Indeed, Jim Burden's plans with Ántonia's sons at the end of *My Ántonia* seem to announce Cather's male-centered novels of the 1920s and their exploration of masculine desire.

While the professor's summers on the lake recall his vacations in Brittany with the Thierault brothers, especially Gaston, "the one he loved best" (105), Cather's details align the setting with a classical heritage. As he swims in the lake, the professor's "head looked sheathed and small and intensely alive, like the heads of the warriors on the Parthenon frieze in their tight, archaic helmets" (71). His classical figure evokes the Sacred Band; the lake itself becomes a sanctuary, both spiritual and erotic space:

> [Tom] and St. Peter were often together in the evening, and on fine afternoons they went swimming. Every Saturday the Professor turned his house over to the cleaning-woman, and he and Tom went to the lake and spent the day in his sail-boat.
>
> It was just the sort of summer St. Peter liked, if he had to be in Hamilton at all. (176)

The pervading mood at the lake is ceremonial. While Grumbach likens it to the Christian ritual of baptism ("A Study" 339), its classical details suggest a Greek athletic or religious event. Swimming in a sacred lake, the professor emerges rejuvenated, afterwards resting in contemplative repose. "Lying by the lake for hours," Rosowski writes, "St. Peter most fully realizes the voice of his unconscious. He gives himself to 'day-dreams' or reveries in which he has 'recognitions' of archetypal truths" (VP 141). Hermione Lee adds that Cather "is involved in the modern quest to find, in the instinctual, the primitive, and the mythological, 'elemental and enduring truths'" (256). In her spiritual search, Cather affirms the ideals of friendship, and they surface in the novel through her treatment of homosexuality.

The landscape at the lake further inspires homoerotic reveries. Tree imagery, especially that of pine trees, appears throughout Cather's prose and fiction. Often it is linked to the sublime, as in her early travel essay written from Lavandou, France:

> There is before the villa a little plateau on the flat top of a cliff extending out into the sea, brown with pine needles, and shaded by one tall, straight pine tree that grows on the very tip of the little promontory. It is good for one's soul to sit there all the day through, wrapped in a steamer rug if the sea breeze blows strong,

and to do nothing for hours together but stare at this great water that seems to trail its delft-blue mantle across the world. Then, as Daudet said, one becomes a part of the foam that drifts, of the wind that blows, and of the pines that answer. (WCIE 158–59)

In *The Professor's House* Cather infuses reverie with arousal, and in doing so, she makes her pine trees part of her modernism, conflating identity and sexuality as well as dreams and desire.[4] Cather's description of the "seven motionless pines" (263), "appliquéd against the blue water," is sensuously Whitmanesque, "their ripe yellow cones, dripping with gum and clustering on the pointed tips like a mass of golden bees in swarming-time" (270). In the course of the novel, they become closely associated with Tom Outland, whether those at the lake, the "grove of pine-trees" (143) beside the physics building, or the "little grove of piñons" (189) on the Blue Mesa. Contemplating the trees at the lake, the professor is also thinking about Tom Outland; as he looks out of his office window at the nearby science laboratory, his memories of his former student and friend are once again stirred by the seductive pines. This emotional penumbra evokes Cather's subtle fusion of form and content, for in literally opening the "square window" (16) of his study, the professor finds his mind filled with thoughts of Tom, thoughts simultaneously joyous and despairing. For at the bottom of his desire, "Truth under all truths" (265), is the knowledge that Tom would never "come back again through the garden door (as he had so often done in dreams!)" (263).

The sacredness of the lake and its engendered landscape extends to other settings in the novel. St. Peter's blue lake mirrors Tom Outland's Blue Mesa and inspires a similar "exaltation" (200) and "religious emotion" (251). Tom and Roddy's "world above the world" (240), where the air is "pure and uncontaminated" (200), also begins to echo gay literary sources, both Pierre Loti's "floating cloister" (*Mon frère Yves* 10) within a "boundless circle" of blue (185) and the "penitential blue" of Walter Pater's sky, "that poetic region between Rome and the sea" (*Marius* 254).

Like the lake, the professor's garden is also part of the view from his study window, and it too is both sacred and erotic space: "His walled-in garden had been the comfort of his life—and it was the one thing his neighbours held against him. He started to make it soon after the birth of his first daughter, when his wife began to be unreasonable about his spending so much time at the lake and on the tennis court" (14). Cather's first description of the garden is also the narrative's first mention of Tom Outland. Opening the door to the professor's garden, as he has once opened the "sky-blue door" (182) of Roddy's room, Tom enters into engendered space. The two men are emotionally linked both with each other and with the garden, for "it was there [St. Peter] and Tom Outland used to sit and talk half through the warm, soft nights" (15). Later descriptions heighten this intimacy. Although St. Peter's orchard is "barren" (52) and nonproductive, evenings spent in the garden with Tom are long and romantic. Enclosed, sensuous, felicitous space, the professor's French garden, like the French woods in *One of Ours*, evokes the pleasures of homosexual pastoral.

The professor's study is perhaps the novel's most engendered space, yet it is in a way different from its other settings. If, as Gaston Bachelard describes in *The Poetics of Space*, "the house allows one to dream in peace" (6), the attic-study offers the professor his most protective shelter. An extension of the house, the attic becomes the place St. Peter loves the most, where he reaches "the utmost depths of revery" (Bachelard 7). More than any other setting, it is inextricably connected with his inner life. It is where he works, but more importantly, it is where he dreams. Both activities are inspired by Tom Outland; indeed, a beloved space, the study is a surrogate for the beloved.

St. Peter expresses this intense attachment in unusual and often unreasonable ways. Although the new house is finished, he continues to rent the old one on the pretense of working in familiar surroundings. The two houses reflect the professor's divided self, his everyday reality and his escape in dreams. "After his university duties were over, he smuggled his bed and clothing back to the old house and settled down to a leisurely bachelor life" (171), a life complete with reveries of Tom Outland. More than any other place, the study is suffused with memories of Tom. Maintaining that space maintains incommunicable feelings; giving it up means surrendering something precious. As Stout explains, "By clinging to his memories and to work that he associated with Tom—his eight-volume history as well as the editing of Tom's diary—St. Peter could cling to the illusion that the great emotion which had once fired his life still remained alive" (93). Unlike the lake and garden, the study is frequented by women, yet Tom's abiding presence is strongly felt, a powerful evocation of Cather's "thing not named." Augusta's sewing forms, with their constant reminders of "certain disappointments" and "cruel biological necessities" (21), have little to do with emotional needs and spiritual desire; keeping them in their accustomed place protects the professor's memories of Tom as well.

Literary allusions sustain Cather's expanding allegory of a Sacred Band and show the strength of her imaginative assimilation of homosexual sources. Paul Comeau observes that Cather's allusive technique is always "to strike one note and then to let the reverberations carry over and blend naturally into the next note" (224). In *The Professor's House* Cather slants her allusions toward homosexuality, and this subtle angling shapes her aesthetics. While reinforcing her classical paradigm, continued allusions to Pierre Loti and Walter Pater, as well as echoes of Marcel Proust, place *The Professor's House* in direct lineage of modern gay literature.

To escape stifling space, Cather metaphorically goes to sea, and through her image of the open window, she evokes the eroticism of Pierre Loti. Echoing her enthusiasm for French fiction, Cather's description of the professor's relationship with Tom Outland as a romance "of the imagination" (258) further invites comparisons between her narrative technique and Loti's male romances. Through the square window of Dutch genre paintings, one sees the masts of ships and feels the seductive lure of the sea; the specificity of "Java" further exoticizes the enticing view. While the masts of ships plying the globe, vacations in Brittany, masculine adventure, and all male-tableaux add a Lotiesque aura to Cather's narrative, this affiliation is nowhere better played out than in St. Peter's seafaring fantasy. Although its beginning is fragmentary, it accrues meaning through repetition and accumulation of detail, changing from a picturesque daydream of shipwrecked sailors into an all-male fantasy in which his wife has no place: "Indeed, nobody was in it but himself, and a weather-dried little sea captain from the Hautes-Pyrénées, half a dozen spry seamen, and a line of gleaming snow peaks, agonizingly high and sharp, along the southern coast of Spain" (95).⁵ Rosowski writes that "Cather found in dreaming a redemption for the human soul" (VP 137) and "turned to dreams as stays against loss and change" (141). In entering the professor's dreams, Cather engenders the most private space of all, and it is here that St. Peter releases the truths of his own heart. "The values that belong to daydreaming mark humanity in its depths," muses Bachelard (6). In *The Professor's House* dreams and reveries are eroticized, and Cather conveys their innermost value through an engendering of intimate space.

Cather's affinity with Walter Pater heightens the homoeroticism of *The Professor's House*. The text's reference to the story of the friendship of Amis and Amile affiliates her with Pater's homosexual aesthetics in *The Renaissance*, where his essay "Two Early French Stories" indirectly places the medieval romance *Li Amitiez de Ami et Amile* in a gay literary context. In Pater's view, this ancient French tale evokes a "free play of human affection" that "makes itself felt in the incidents of a great friendship, a friendship pure and generous, pushed to a sort of passionate exaltation, and more than faithful unto death" (R 8). Assigning the story an erotic intensity, Pater affirms his own views about homosexuality and cultural formation, and its position in *The Renaissance* confirms the centrality of those views to his art.⁶ While Cather's professor explains to his wife the refinement of manners in the Middle Ages, the male chivalry of Amis and Amile broadens his sensibility and obliquely colors his cultural observations.

Cather blends the erotic possibilities of *Li Amitiez de Ami et Amile* into the male stories of *The Professor's House*. Investing Tom's Indian blanket with talismanic power, Kathleen likens it to the wooden cups that always revealed the knights to one another: "Kathleen stroked it thoughtfully. 'Roddy brought it up from Old Mexico, you know. He gave it to Tom that winter he had pneumonia. Tom ought to have taken it to France with him. He used to say that Rodney Blake might turn up in the Foreign Legion. If he had taken this, it might have been like the wooden cups that were always revealing *Amis* and *Amile* to each other'" (130–31). The wooden cups possess sacramental value and seal the knights' friendship with the ritual of communion. Tom's blanket also has spiritual power and, like the cups, charges romantic friendship with erotic feelings. Paralleling his attachment to the attic-study, St. Peter displays similar feelings for Tom's gift and emphatically confesses to his daughter that "Nothing could part me from that blanket" (130). Its presence in his study—its very color, odor, and texture—embodies Tom's spirit. Likewise, the presence of the eroticized French legend in *The Professor's House* subtly evokes the homoeroticism of Cather's text, as the legend's inclusion in *The Renaissance* conveys Pater's homosexual critique.

Pater's *Marius the Epicurean* further informs Cather's exploration of male friendship. "In that novel," Brian Reade writes, "it will be noted how male friendships were among the more powerful emotions described; and not only were these dependent on physical attractiveness and therefore strictly erotic, but they were linked dramatically to religious crises" (20). Cather's narrative also confronts crisis, both physical and spiritual. For most of the novel, St. Peter is an epicure, enjoying a life of sensations and ideas: "If a thing gave him delight, he got it, if he sold his shirt for it. By doing without many so-called necessities he had managed to have his luxuries" (27). His personal pleasures all reveal the "aesthetic charm" (R xii) of a Paterian sensibility: his meals are carefully prepared, his habits are orderly, and his thoughts and impressions are cultivated and refined.

Marius the Epicurean, like *The Professor's House*, progresses through the dynamics of male friendship and masculine desire. As Richmond Crinkley points out, "Physical love seldom becomes overt in Pater, but throughout his writings one finds an intense preoccupation with male physical beauty. The suggestiveness of much of Pater makes some readers uneasy, but to ignore it or to pretend it does not exist would be an evasion of the obvious" (146).[7] Marius's attraction to the youth Flavian and later to the soldier Cornelius is as much physical as it is emotional, and like the professor at the conclusion of Cather's novel, Marius is caught between conflicted modes of thought—epicurian delight and stoical restraint.

If the idea of homosexuality is Cather's "thing not named," how does the text accommodate its unstated presence? Cather's fictional experiments in *The Professor's House* resemble Professor Crane's experiments in the laboratory; both explore the "extent of space" (141)—he its physical reach, she its imaginative possibilities. By engendering narrative space, Cather allies homosexuality to her text in a fusion of form and content Jacob Stockinger defines as "homotexual" (135).[8]

Sexuality's most vital textual role in *The Professor's House* is its connection with creativity. For example, St. Peter's book, *Spanish Adventurers in North America*, is tantalizingly erotic, from its conception to its execution and completion. He conceives its form while daydreaming aboard the *L'Espoir*: "That summer Charles kept him for three weeks in his oleander-buried house in the Prado, until his little brig, *L'Espoir*, sailed out of the new port with a cargo for Algeciras. The captain was from the Haute-Pyrénées, and his spare crew were all Provençals, seamen trained in that hard school of the Gulf of Lyons. On the voyage everything seemed to feed the plan of the work that was forming in St. Peter's mind; the skipper, the old Catalan second mate, the sea itself" (105–06).

The sailors, the sea, and the spectacular setting join together to engender creative desire:

One day stood out above the others. All day long they were skirting the south coast of Spain; from the rose of dawn to the gold of sunset the ranges of the Sierra Nevadas towered on their right, snow peak after snow peak, high beyond the flight of fancy, gleaming like crystal and topaz. St. Peter lay looking up at them from a little boat riding low in the purple water, and the design of his book unfolded in the air above him, just as definitely as the mountain ranges themselves. And the design was sound. He had accepted it as inevitable, had never meddled with it, and it had seen him through. (106)

Here Cather provides the background to the professor's fantasy. Both the dream and the reality linger in his mind as a powerful recollection of personal happiness and imaginative inspiration. St. Peter's Spanish adventure precipitates his own "voyage perilous" and, in doing so, implicitly connects sexuality with the "ineffable origin" (Edward and Lillian Bloom 124) of creativity.[9]

St. Peter's stories of male pioneering are so firmly linked to his own experiences that "to him, the most important chapters of his history were interwoven with personal memories" (101). An emotional overlapping of the professor's reveries conveys this continuity between his personal life and the life of his book as a recollection of his skirting the coast of Spain all day long evocatively resembles his memory of sailing with Tom Outland on Saturday afternoons. Tom also inspires completion of its later volumes, the part in which the professor comes closest to his real self. The results of this psychic self-possession are spiritually liberating: "When the whole plan of his narrative was coming clearer and clearer all the time, when he could feel his hand growing easier with his material, when all the foolish conventions about that kind of writing were falling away and his relation with his work was becoming every day more simple, natural, and happy,—he cared as little as the Spanish Adventurers themselves what Professor So-and-So thought about them" (32–33). St. Peter's spontaneous narrative creates an identity both genuine and true; indeed, its history is his own. If he and his book were becoming "simple and inevitable" (258), it was because of Tom Outland. "Because there were children, and fervour in the blood and brain, books were born as well as daughters" (265). Echoing Plato's concept of spiritual procreation, the professor's eight-volume history is also his progeny, his "splendid Spanish-adventurer sons!" (165), the product of his friendship with Tom Outland.[10] And like Cather's experimental novel, the professor's own "experiment" (33) in writing exudes a homoerotic impulse, attested to by the growing interest his book arouses in young men scattered across the United States and England as well as the deep impressions it makes upon Tom Outland. In this sense, the response to *Spanish Adventurers in North America* resembles the excitement felt in England by John Addington Symonds and Edward Carpenter over Whitman's *Leaves of Grass* and the special interest some Victorian readers, including Oscar Wilde, took in Pater's *The Renaissance*; even Cather's own enthusiasm for Housman's *A Shropshire Lad* shares these close and ardent affinities.

If homoeroticism creates a sense of self in *The Professor's House*, Cather's metaphor of homosexuality paradoxically dramatizes the dilemma of self-identity. Mirroring the homosexual's inability to live openly in a disapproving society, a muting of feeling suffuses the novel with a sense of alienation and despair and intensifies its pervasive air of secrecy. Silences also inform the texts residing within *The Professor's House*. For example, in Cather's unfurnishing process, as Love writes, "there is the capacity for enlarged feeling" (305), exemplified by the latent power of "Tom Outland's Story" and the stylistic distinction of Tom's diary. Although both works lack overt erotic force, Tom's experience of the mesa is sexually charged, and it is in Cather's and Tom's restraint that strong feelings are evoked.

Tom and Roddy's life together echoes the male pioneering of *Spanish Adventurers* and the professor's own adventures in writing it. Tom and Roddy "live an idyllic existence of male comradeship and love, the familiar male pair that frontier American literature has often glorified" (Grumbach, "A Study" 340–41). Their early experiences revolve around tenderness and trust; as Tom was interested in Roddy and devoted to his care, so too was Roddy equally solicitous of Tom's well-being. A ten-year age difference endows their relationship with the classical sanction of the Sacred Band. And like the spry French sailors in the professor's fantasy, even old Harry is "a castaway Englishman" (196) who together with Tom and Roddy "made a happy family" (198).

Describing the Cliff City, Tom Outland focuses on its central tower, the "fine thing" (201) that held the parts together. Friendship, like the tower, is the "fine thing" engendering Tom's experience of the Blue Mesa. Alone with his beloved, Tom knows happiness; merely alone, he suffers despair and remorse: "But the older I grow, the more I understand what it was I did that night on the mesa. Anyone who requites faith and friendship as I did, will have to pay for it. I'm not very sanguine about good fortune for myself. I'll be called to account when I least expect it" (253). Departing from the legend of Amis and Amile, Cather explores the consequences of that loss and betrayal. The two knights' fidelity provides an instructive contrast to Tom and Roddy's broken friendship. While Love writes that "The mesa will be, of course, the scene of Tom's great discovery and his great loss" (304), Cather's technique blurs Tom's experience, and readers are never quite sure whether Tom's "discovery" and "loss" is Roddy Blake or the Blue Mesa. Cather conflates the two, and this indeterminacy heightens the novel's ambiguity. What readers feel in Tom's story resembles what the professor feels when editing his diary; both responses mirror feelings elicited by Cather's "novel démeublé," for in enriching the narrative power of *The Professor's House*, sexual aesthetics enhance its embedded texts as well.

While Lee admits that "It is tempting to interpret [the professor's] true self as a homosexual feeling for Tom," she argues that a homosexual interpretation "doesn't quite accommodate the novel's obscure sense of spiritual dislocation" (240–41). But *The Professor's House* is as much about spiritual recovery as it is about spiritual loss. Platonic friendship engenders such renewal, and through male friendship St. Peter discovers a sense of self in accord with his "inclination," "instinctive conviction" (269), and "attitude of mind" (282). And this is precisely the redemptive value of Cather's Sacred Band. "Art and religion (they are the same thing, in the end, of course) have given man the only happiness he has ever had" (69), St. Peter passionately professes to his students. Investing facts with imaginative excitement reiterates the Paterian cadence of Cather's text. Indeed, critiquing the history of culture and civilization, St. Peter resembles eminent Victorian lecturers such as Pater himself; writing his eight-volume history further recalls Pater's writing *The History of the Renaissance*. Of St. Peter's philosophy, Rosowski states: "He recognizes that we need aesthetics to provide order against the chaos of nature and the vastness of time. Nature gains from being arranged, he reflects, and we are happiest when ritual arranges our individual lives, so that each action occurs not in a void but within a larger meaning" (VP 136). The ritual of friendship in *The Professor's House* provides such redemptive, imaginative space.

Such a reading raises a crucial question about Cather's narration, however. Stout asks, "Why did she project these complex feelings in the form of a male, rather than a female character?" (90). Cather's affiliation with the homosexual literary tradition moves readers beyond conventional answers—such as Cather's "old feelings about the masculinity of art" and "her sense of France as the home of a great but essentially masculine artistic culture" (Stout 90)—and offers a new assessment of Cather's motivation. In *The Professor's House* Cather sustains a platonic paradigm begun in *One of Ours* and extending through *Death Comes for the Archbishop* in which homosexuality is linked to spirituality. Her symbolic appropriation of the Sacred Band prescribes a male protagonist, and Cather draws upon her gift of sympathy to meet this artistic demand.

While friendship offers spiritual happiness, its absence creates despair. Echoes of Marcel Proust deepen the despairing mood of *The Professor's House*. While Lee likens Cather's style to Proust's complexity, Jo Ann Middleton adds that Cather "bows to Marcel

Proust" (106) in her modernity. Part of this modernity is the dilemma of homosexuality—its capacity for happiness and its certainty of despair. Lee discerns this melancholy in Tom's remark about Roddy's solicitude: "He ought to have had boys of his own to look after. Nature's full of such substitutions, but they always seem to me sad, even in botany" (185–86). What Lee interprets as "Cather's most direct reference to homosexual feeling in her fiction" (250) in my view merely enhances the novel's Proustian mood.

Indirection tells a different story, and Cather's sexual aesthetics rejuvenate a sometimes melancholy narrative voice. Again the metaphor of homosexuality encodes both happiness and despair, and Cather's text oscillates between the two. For instance, male friendship mitigates the "remedial influence" (280) of Augusta's story. Stout argues that St. Peter's sewing woman "represents woman as sustainer, as caretaker" and "answers to St. Peter's deepest need, his will to live" (91). Tom, on the other hand, represents the professor's intense need to live with delight. Both are corrective forces and exert redemptive power: quoting the *Aeneid*, Tom is Cather's classical spirit; quoting the Bible, Augusta is her Christian strength. Together Cather's Magnificat and her Sacred Band create an ongoing dialogue between spiritual philosophies, stressing at the same time the dialectics between Christian and classical myth at work in *The Professor's House*.

Augusta's stoical approach to life sharply contrasts with the professor's epicurean habits, and the end of the novel echoes the interplay of Christian and classical myths concluding *Marius the Epicurean*. For both Cather and Pater, sexual ambiguity is linked to spiritual uncertainty. Acquiescing to a stoical philosophy, Cather's epicure seems resigned to a life without delight: "His temporary release from consciousness seemed to have been beneficial. He had let something go—and it was gone: something very precious, that he could not consciously have relinquished, probably. . . . He thought he knew where he was, and that he could face with fortitude the *Berengaria* and the future" (282–83). Although the word "certain" appears with unusual frequency in the early chapters of *The Professor's House*, here Cather's language betrays an unsettling element of doubt and disillusionment. Consequently, the final certainty that "There was still Augusta, however; a world full of Augustas, with whom one was outward bound" (281) seems half-hearted and unconvincing. Rather than sailing for Java or Spain or "Outland's country" (270), "outward bound" with Augusta means "fac[ing] with fortitude the *Berengaria* and the future." As Alice Bell notes, the ship *Berengaria* invokes a significant historical parallel: Berengaria of Navarre was the wife of King Richard I, to whom he grudgingly returned after experiencing a liberating homosexual interlude (121). The professor could once face a family dinner only after reminiscing about Tom Outland or his youthful adventures in France with the Thierault brothers; that fortifying impulse, however, is now gone.

While homoerotic desire reconciles the tension in the professor's life, his renunciation of these feelings creates a life "without delight. . . . without joy, without passionate griefs" (282). Rosowski's argument that the something precious he has relinquished is the "lover"—"the outward-reaching impulse to unite with an object" (vp 138)—is a particularly apt metaphor for St. Peter's relationship with Tom Outland in its evocation of passionate friendship and emotional desire. As Grumbach further explains, "The novel, like its hero, is reconciled at the end, to the human impossibility of being one's true self, of achieving 'natural' happiness outside the social stringencies of marriage and family, indeed, of heterosexual love" ("A Study" 343). Homosexuality poignantly evokes this tension, conveying concealed emotions and the suppression of desire.

"Ambiguity lies at the heart of *The Professor's House*," Rosowski argues, "and therein lies its brilliance" (vp 139). While not resolving its ambiguities, Cather's aesthetics engage readers with its uncertainties and the paradox of "sad pleasure" (266). As the narrative shifts between past and present, so too does Cather's technique explore both happiness and despair; indeed, while sexual aesthetics engender hope, they also evoke a somber discovery of self. Like the woods that eventually change into a "dark clump of pine-trees" (89–90), Cather's imagery darkens and becomes joyless. Once a formidable and tireless swimmer, the professor seems as much panic-stricken as surefooted at the conclusion of the novel. When the window closes, the attic no longer offers escape; when it is re-opened, rather than liberating, eroticized space, St. Peter faces a life of "conventional gestures" (261) and stifling American propriety. Letting go with the heart means surrendering the spirit as well; such is the professor's future without the "glittering idea" embodied by Tom Outland and engendered on the Blue Mesa. "Desire is creation" (29) Cather insists in *The Professor's House;* its absence dulls the spirit. Indifference, resignation, and a sad heart end *The Professor's House* as ambiguously as it began.

6

Spiritual Friendship in *Death Comes for the Archbishop*

WHILE most readers feel that *Death Comes for the Archbishop* (1927) is a deeply religious book, few recognize the contribution homosexuality makes to its spiritual mood. As she does in *One of Ours* and *The Professor's House*, Cather again depicts male friendship in a largely male environment; however, the religious background of *Death Comes for the Archbishop* brings to the text a narrative dimension missing in the earlier fiction. Describing the novel's genesis in a letter to *Commonweal*, Cather writes: "The longer I stayed in the Southwest, the more I felt that the story of the Catholic Church in that country was the most interesting of all its stories" ("On *Death*" 5). The way she tells that particular story makes it the most intriguing of her male-centered fiction. As her homosexual paradigm reaches its spiritual potential, *Death Comes for the Archbishop* becomes the apotheosis of Cather's Sacred Band.

Discussions of the novel inevitably echo the language of friendship. Merrill Maguire Skaggs observes that in *Death Comes for the Archbishop*, "Cather recovers her faith in friendship" (19). Cather herself speaks of the prototype for her main character as "a sort of invisible personal friend" ("On *Death*" 7). Extending this analogy, Hermione Lee writes that "Cather always had a sense of loss and regret after finishing a book, as though parting company for ever from a close friend" (289). And in an analysis of Cather's evocative style, Susan J. Rosowski argues that "As much as the friendship between Latour and Vaillant, the narrator establishes the happy mood of the book: he takes the reader with him as a companion on a journey of storytelling" (VP 169).

The stories Cather tells in *Death Comes for the Archbishop* are profoundly religious. Simple stories become parables of faith, and minor details assume spiritual significance. While such stories often erode the novel's erotic texture, it is here that Cather's treatment of homosexuality reveals the nature of her achievement. Linking homosexuality with the early history of the Catholic Church, John Boswell states that "There is in fact a considerable body of evidence to suggest that homosexual relations were especially associated with the clergy" (CSTH 187). "Even popes," Boswell adds, "were not above such accusations, and in some areas the mere fact of having taken orders seems to have rendered one liable to the suspicion of being a 'sodomite'" (217–18).[1] Given this historical context, the very subject of Cather's novel indirectly intimates homosexuality. Cather underscores this affiliation by identifying the formal sources of her design: the saints' lives and the religious murals of Puvis de Chavannes ("On *Death*" 9). The combined effect of these influences makes *Death Comes for the Archbishop* "feel like a medieval legend" (Lee 271), an impression implicitly heightened by Cather's treatment of homosexuality.

Returning to the recent past for her story and recalling a more distant past in its narration, Cather does more than tell the story of the Catholic Church in the Southwest, and her utilization of the historical novel underscores this complexity. Connecting the historical genre with homosexuality, Ian Young points out that "Tales set in eras when homosexual relationships were more accepted or less suspect than in the present have provided a variety of authors with opportunities for treating homosexual attachments matter-of-factly or even idealistically. A historical setting can enable readers— and writers!—to overcome what resistance they may have toward homosexuality in a contemporary context" ("The Flower" 158). Cather's combination of history and narrative provides both a setting congenial to her friendship theme and a form conducive to its telling. Comparing *Death Comes for the Archbishop* with the partisan manner of William Howlett's *Life of Bishop Machebeuf,* Lee writes that "Nothing could be further from Cather's impartial, apolitical tone. Her appropriation of this, the latest of her male authorities, is all in the direction of suggestiveness and evocation, away from propaganda and orthodoxy" (267). Sexual ambiguity creates an elusive text and ultimately helps Cather make Howlett's story her own.

An early scene establishes the correlation between Cather's sexual aesthetics and "the thing not named." Awakened in Santa Fe by the morning Angelus, Bishop Latour is imaginatively inspired by its silvery tone: "Full, clear, with something bland and suave, each note floated through the air like a globe of silver. Before the nine strokes were done Rome faded, and behind it he sensed something Eastern, with palm trees,—Jerusalem, perhaps, though he had never been there. Keeping his eyes closed, he cherished for a moment this sudden, pervasive sense of the East" (43). As the fourteenth-century Spanish bell reveals its oriental craftsmanship, so too does it evoke the novel's narrative method; as it sounds its exotic notes to Latour's discerning ears, it likewise presents to the reader the erotic undertones of Cather's text.

This scene also announces Cather's most pervasive strategy, that of intermingling narrative elements: earth and sky, history and fiction, sexuality and spirituality are blended together as are the gold and silver of the Spanish bell. Among the most perfectly fused elements in *Death Comes for the Archbishop* are art and religion. Throughout the text the ideals of the "novel démeublé" are indistinguishable from those of religious faith. Latour's definition of miracles illustrates this textual fusion: "The Miracles of the Church seem to me to rest not so much upon faces or voices or healing power coming suddenly near to us from afar off, but upon our perceptions being made finer, so that for a moment our eyes can see and our ears can hear what is there about us always" (50).

Whether in the form of miracles or memories, incommunicable feelings and intangible impressions abound in *Death Comes for the Archbishop*, further evoking Cather's fusion of art and religion.

Homosexuality adds another element to Cather's narrative interplay and exists in *Death Comes for the Archbishop* as perhaps the most provocative presence of "the thing not named." John J. Murphy observes that the Acoma legend of Fray Baltazar "is a compendium of most of the excesses of the native clergy" ("Willa Cather's Archbishop" 263), including "political intrigue, gambling, hoarding money and siring children" (259). Scattered details in the text imply other transgressions. In the prologue, set in Rome, the dinner guests of Cardinal de Allande describe the New World clergy as "dissolute" (8), and in Santa Fe, "lewd" children are chastised for "speak[ing] filth against the priests" (216). Kit Carson admits to his early thinking that all priests were "rascals" and nuns "bad women" and adds that "A good many of the native priests here bear out that story" (76). In his personal letters Machebeuf admonishes the native clergy as "scandalous beyond description" (quoted in Howlett 164) and registers disgust at the "atrocious accusations and insulting reflections" (Howlett 193) charged by rival priests against himself and Bishop Lamy. Providing a broader historical outline, Boswell states: "Many pagan writers objected to Christianity precisely because of what they claimed was sexual looseness on the part of its adherents, and much Christian apologetic was aimed at defending Christians against the common belief that they were given to every form of sexual indulgence—including homosexual acts. This belief seems to have been at least partly rooted in fact" (CSTH 131).

Such "facts" are missing in *Death Comes for the Archbishop*, and Cather's omission draws attention to a curious gap between church history and the novel's historical framework. In reprimanding the native priests for their "sensual disturbance[s]" (145), the text seeks to curb every indulgence except homosexuality. Indeed, while "Carnal commerce" (106) with women is easily available and frequently mentioned, nothing is specifically said of homosexual relations; while they are vaguely implied, they remain categorically un-named and undenounced.

What is the meaning of Cather's silence? Is she being evasive or merely exercising delicacy and restraint? Or is her discretion an-other "strategy of reticence"? The answer lies, I believe, in Cather's sexual aesthetics, her evocation of homosexuality to sug-gest "the thing not named." To disparage homosexuality would disparage her art and, more importantly, diminish the emotional relationship at the center of *Death Comes for the Archbishop*. As if to avoid this contradiction, Cather spiritualizes the friendship be-tween Latour and Vaillant, and their relationship, like their voca-tion, assumes a vow of intimacy without sexuality. Celibacy, how-ever, does more than circumvent physiology; it transcends the physical and becomes Cather's paradigm for spiritual love.

Although Cather creates a "deliberately chaste book" (Lee 285), she simultaneously encodes an ambiguously erotic text. Spiritual friendship itself is foregrounded in a theology that combines relig-ious feelings with physical affection. Tradition is very much a part of Latour's "imaginative intelligence" (Edward and Lillian Bloom 210), and *Death Comes for the Archbishop* values inherited traditions such as cooking, craftsmanship, and Catholicism. Boswell de-scribes another heritage that is very much a part of the novel's in-clusiveness: "It is indeed too often overlooked that just as there was a pagan ascetic and antierotic tradition, so was there a Christian tradition of tolerant and positive attitudes toward love and eroti-cism" (CSTH 163). Cather's "mixed theology" (31) explores this du-ality as when Latour and Martínez argue over clerical celibacy. Cather discreetly opens their debate to include intense friendships between priests, perhaps what Martínez means when he refers to "French fashions" (148). Of Cather's background in theology, her friend Edith Lewis writes that "all her life she had been profoundly interested in Catholicism—especially in the Catholicism of the Middle Ages, of the time of Abelard and St. Bernard. She had read widely on the subject long before she came to write the *Archbishop*" (147). While Cather specifically mentions St. Augustine and his prohibitive doctrines, the narrative indirectly summons more tolerant Christian thinkers such as St. Anselm of Bec (1033–1109), later archbishop of Canterbury, and St. Aelred of Rievaulx (1109–67), known as the English St. Bernard, perhaps the most influential writers in the medieval tradition of passionate friendship.

Cather transmutes this theological tradition into literature. As she was interested in the daily life of such a man as Lamy, so too do the lives of men like Anselm and Aelred inform her narrative. While Anselm was the first who "in his generation groped for words to express the intensity of his feelings for his friends" (Southern 34), it is Aelred's views expressed in treatises like *Spiritual Friendship* and *The Mirror of Charity* that expand the similarities between Cather's text and the lives of the saints. Aelred emphasizes affection as a means of approaching divine love and finds in friendship a correlation between physical and spiritual experience. It was Aelred, Boswell writes, who "gave love between those of the same gender its most profound and lasting expressions in a Christian context" (CSTH 221).[2]

Aelred announces his central theme in the opening of *Spiritual Friendship*: "Here we are, you and I, and I hope a third, Christ, is in our midst" (51). Echoing St. John, he stresses that "he that abides in friendship, abides in God, and God in him" (66). Like St. Aelred, Cather is interested in approaching divine love and posits friendship as a path toward its realization. The search for the ideal friend in *One of Ours* leads to the idealized friendship in *Death Comes for the Archbishop*, a relationship that fictionally renders Aelred's teaching that "God is Friendship" (65).

As friendship was an essential part of religious life for men like Anselm and Aelred, Cather builds her narrative around male friendship and its spiritual ideals. Latour and Vaillant, Eusabio and Latour, Vaillant and Revardy, Lucero and Martínez, Latour and Bernard, Antonio Olivares and Manuel Chavez—all fortify the text with the strength of their affections. The latter's story sounds the tone of Cather's narration. As a youth, Chavez was left for dead while on an Indian raiding party. Pierced by arrows, "one shaft clear through his body" (185), and suffering from hunger and thirst, he walked two days and nights before finding food and water, finally collapsing "under two noble oak trees" (186). As a prosperous rancher, the elegantly handsome Chavez boasts that his aristocratic ancestors include two Castilian knights who liberated the city of Chavez from the Moors in the twelfth century. In its emphasis on physical endurance, this inset story resembles the English boy's experience in *One of Ours*. The two ancestral knights evoke the medieval friendship of Amis and Amile as well as Cather's other male pairs, and their liberation of Chavez echoes the liberation of Athens by Harmodius and Aristogiton, the martyred lovers of antiquity.[3] The arrows add a religious aura to Chavez's history, recalling the crucifixion of Christ and the suffering of St. Sebastian, the sacrificial saint of gay iconology. Chavez's unmatched skill with the bow further evokes St. Sebastian, the "patron of archers" (Woods 28) whose symbol is an arrow.[4]

As in the romances of Pierre Loti and the prose of Walter Pater, Cather's stories of male friendship depict the intermingled erotic, emotional, and spiritual relationships of her characters. The narrative style of a legend accommodates this ambiguity: "In *The Golden Legend* the martyrdoms of the saints are no more dwelt upon than are the trivial incidents of their lives; it is as though all human experiences, measured against one supreme spiritual experience, were of about the same importance. The essence of such writing is not to hold the note, not to use an incident for all there is in it—but to touch and pass on" (Cather, "On *Death*" 9). The unaccented style of a legend merely suggests and then moves on, as the Indians move across their country, in unhurried flight. "In this kind of writing," Cather continues, "the mood is the thing" ("On *Death*" 10), and the mood of *Death Comes for the Archbishop*, to use her words in the novel, is one of "extraordinary personal devotion" (289).

Religion engenders the text of Cather's novel, and in a crude frontier society, it maintains a link between men and their humanity. The gift of Christianity is its sympathy, and Cather's protagonists respond to the humanizing influences of Catholicism. Her central male characters either resemble biblical patriarchs or recall the apostles of Christ. Rather than emasculating them, their religious feelings, however feminine, broaden their masculinity. Although later "misguided" (293), Kit Carson is compassionate throughout much of the narrative, Eusabio is respectful and courteous, Luzon is generous, and even the young murderer about to hang is gentle and tender-hearted, spending his last hours in solicitous devotion to Santiago. As has often been remarked, Latour is Cather's quintessential hero—in Lee's words, "delicate and distinguished, chivalric, aesthetic, sympathetic (especially to the Indians, for whom Howlett has no time at all), nostalgic for France, in love with order and tradition, patient to the point of passivity, vulnerable, self-doubting, and in need of Vaillant's support" (268). His "broad sympathies" (Brown 264) and "attitude of acceptance" (Rosowski, VP 163) make him the perfect embodiment of Cather's imagination. This same sensitivity makes him the ideal expression of her art.

Details of Latour and Vaillant's friendship further reveal Cather's sexual aesthetics. Physical affection and spiritual ardor are perfectly blended; their love for one another is identical to their love of the Catholic Church. As boys at school, Latour chooses Vaillant, a "homely," "queer lad" (224), to be his friend, thus beginning a lifelong companionship. As Aelred teaches in *Spiritual Friendship*, the progression of friendship through selection, testing, and acceptance imitates religious training; faith and friendship intermingle as choosing a friend mirrors knowing God. In dramatizing Vaillant's personal struggle to break the ties of blood and country and become a missionary priest, Cather conflates spiritual and emotional crises by placing a "higher trust" (204) in faith and friendship alike. Latour and Vaillant's departure from their native Auvergne has all the anguish and excitement of a romantic elopement, and their friendship is as suggestive of a marriage as is the relationship between Christ and St. John. Vaillant's signet ring, later worn by Latour, signifies their deep emotional commitment to each other and to God.

In one sense Cather's story of the Catholic Church reflects the historical and cultural shift from Hellenism to Christianity. As Mary Ruth Ryder points out, by the time she wrote *Death Comes for the Archbishop* "Cather would increasingly describe human struggles in religious terms, never abandoning the allusions from classical myth which were such an integral part of her thought, but subordinating those images to a larger dimension of Christian allegory" (248). In addition, *Death Comes for the Archbishop* demonstrates both Cather's artistic interest in Catholicism and its connection with her aesthetics. "It can be argued," writes Brian Reade, "that the Roman Church had greater attractions than any Protestant Church for the homosexual—both male and female—in that its theology and teaching were not based on empirical studies of the Bible" (8). The Roman Church's notion of divine love especially appealed to Cather's imagination and was "the most important single idea she took from Catholicism" (Rosowski, VP 164).

As Cather's gift of sympathy reflects her experience of divine love, homosexuality reflects its imaginative possibilities. With its absence of a central female character and its emphasis on Mariology and the Virgin birth, *Death Comes for the Archbishop* appears to be a sexless narrative or at least a text in which sexuality seems carefully contained. Lee writes that "There is only one, strange, underground threat to the novel's tranquil sublimation of sexual repression or anxiety into Mariolatry" (286)—"the successful sublimation of its underground sexual feeling is centred on . . . the Virgin Mother, Mary" (285). However, Cather places a parallel emphasis on Christ, and as Thomas M. Casey points out, Cather's Christology "needs to be understood if we are to make sense of certain sections of the narrative" (25). As Cather evokes an image of Mary as "a goddess who should yet be a woman" (257), so too does the text implicitly envision a humanized Christ: Latour feels the "Presence" (256) of Christ when he is alone in his study; and throughout *Death Comes for the Archbishop* the closeness of a divine companion is a component of spiritual friendship.

A Christ-centered narrative can contain significant homosexual implications. In the context of the aesthetic movement, for example, "to embrace the faith is to be embraced by Jesus," and Victorian writers such as Gerald Manly Hopkins found in Catholicism a means to release sublimated sexual and emotional desire (Woods 47).[5] And while Gregory Woods argues that "the theme of Christ's homosexuality is periodically recurrent" (46), Boswell explains why this is so:

> Sexuality appears to have been largely a matter of indifference to Jesus. . . . He pronounced no condemnations of sexuality among the unmarried and said nothing which bore any relation to homosexuality. The only sexual issue of importance to Jesus appears to have been fidelity: he did not mention the procreation or rearing of children in connection with marriage but only its permanence, and he prohibited divorce except in cases of infidelity. He was apparently celibate himself, and the only persons with whom the Gospels suggest he had any special relationship were men, especially Saint John, who carefully describes himself throughout his gospel as the disciple whom Jesus loved. (CSTH 114–15)[6]

Whereas gay feelings are conducive to this kind of love, the sexual ambiguities in Cather's text evince a similar sensibility, reminiscent of both Christ and his followers and other biblical stories of same-sex relationships.[7]

Spiritual friendship sets the tone for all else in *Death Comes for the Archbishop*. Rosowski writes: "the friendship of the two priests is one of great love, the major example of the mood that unifies the narrative and the miracles that run through it" (VP 163). Everything, including eroticism, is seemingly subsumed by spiritual devotion. In a narrative strategy akin to the ritual of transubstantiation, passion is changed into pity, and sexual energy is transmuted into spiritual desire. Just as Latour sees the spiritual beauty of Vaillant, they both see the inner beauty of those around them—Jacinto's fine manners and Magdalena's radiance, for example. The landscape itself evokes "a religious silence" (151). Conspicuously missing in this text is the purely physical beauty of a Julio, Cather's young Mexican guide and the inspiration for much of the sensuality associated with the Southwest in her earlier fiction.[8] Nor is there a physical male image of such evocative power as that of Tom Outland in *The Professor's House* or the luminous English boy in *One of Ours*. El Greco's portrait of an effeminate "St. Francis in meditation" (12) comes closest to these earlier examples of masculine beauty. Yet while sexuality and spirituality are equally rendered in that androgynous portrait, its erotic attraction is diminished by its spiritual appeal.

Other details enlarge this pattern. Lucero's boastful joke ridiculing Martínez's declining vitality underscores the elimination of sexuality from the text: "'You see how it is,' Padre Lucero would say to the young men at a wedding party, 'my way is better than old José Martínez's. His nose and chin are getting to be close neighbours now, and a petticoat is not much good to him any more. But I can still rise upright at the sight of a dollar. With a new piece of money in my hand I am happier than ever; and what can he do with a pretty girl but regret?'" (161). Cather's unruly horses in *One of Ours*, Pompey and Satan, become affectionate mules in *Death Comes for the Archbishop*, symbols of Latour and Vaillant's emotional intimacy. Even the Spanish names heard throughout the text defuse sexuality with their spiritual lull: Contento, Angelica, Tranquilino.

Cather reinforces her relaxed narrative manner by describing her experience of writing *Death Comes for the Archbishop* as "a happy vacation from life" ("On *Death*" 11). An early scene in the novel sets this rhythm in motion. As Latour rides into Santa Fe for the first time, the narrator observes that "The long main street began at the church, the town seemed to flow from it like a stream from a spring" (22). Subsequent imagery sustains this mood as everywhere the text emphasizes release: underground water bursts through the desert's floor, old Sada is released from spiritual bondage, Magdalena is saved from a brutal marriage, images of keys abound, cities are liberated, and animals are set free. Near the end of the novel, the abolition of black slavery and the return of exiled Navajos to their traditional homeland reemphasize Cather's pattern of spiritual freedom. A perpetual flowering—such as that associated with the miracle of Our Lady of Guadalupe and the verdant meadows of Arroyo Hondo and the Canyon de Chelly—intensifies the novel's renunciation of sex. No longer the protective space of homosexual pastoral, Cather's flower imagery now provides a spiritual refuge, "an Indian Garden of Eden" (297).

But even as it renounces sex, Cather's text avows a sexual impulse. The rhythm of the novel is both spiritual and physical, its language simultaneously chaste and erotic, spontaneous and controlled. Yet while Cather's flexible idiom combines sexuality and storytelling (the text begins with "climax" and ends in "release"), her "primary ecstasy" (Sergeant 229) remains a flowering of spiritual desire. Always traveling, a physical and spiritual voyager, Latour is frequently presented waking up in the early morning, the physical counterpart to the awakening of the spirit. Cather's central metaphor for spiritual freedom is death itself, the release from life—"a dramatic climax, a moment when the soul made its entrance into the next world, passing in full consciousness through a lowly door to an unimaginable scene" (170).

The dramatic conclusion of *Death Comes for the Archbishop* is a climax not only of Latour's life but also of the images of release shaping the narrative: "Something soft and wild and free, something that whispered to the ear on the pillow, lightened the heart, softly, softly picked the lock, slid the bolts, and released the prisoned spirit of man into the wind, into the blue and gold, into the morning, into the morning!" (276). Throughout this description, physical signs communicate spiritual growth. As in Cather's most provocative passages elsewhere, an indeterminate "something" here again tantalizes a reader. The "something oriental" (45) that Latour senses in the Spanish bell anticipates the "something soft and wild and free" in the exhilarating morning air; indeed, the "something that whispered to the ear on the pillow" awakens the eroticism of the desert landscape.

Loretta Wasserman attributes Wallace Stevens's praise of Cather's style to her mature handling of sexual themes ("The Lovely

Storm" 357). Intimations of homosexuality reflect this sophistication. While patterns of male friendship in *Death Comes for the Archbishop* participate in the homosocial/homosexual continuum of mainstream American literature—especially the Western tradition of Owen Wister and James Fenimore Cooper—underpinnings of "extraordinary personal devotion" affiliate Cather's text with distinctly gay themes, from the Greek ideal of a Sacred Band to Whitman's "adhesiveness" and "love of comrades" ("For You O Democracy," LG 117). Kinship with Walter Pater's homosexual aesthetics firmly establishes *Death Comes for the Archbishop* within this literary tradition. As do her allusions to Amis and Amile in *The Professor's House*, here the names Marius (*Marius the Epicurean*) and Latour (*Gaston de Latour*) endow Cather's text with a Paterian resonance. But the most striking correspondence is the similarity between Cather's climactic passage and the controversial conclusion of Pater's *Studies in the History of the Renaissance*: "While all melts under our feet, we may well catch at any exquisite passion, or any contribution to knowledge that seems, by a lifted horizon, to set the spirit free for a moment, or any stirring of the senses, strange dyes, strange flowers, and curious odours, or work of the artist's hands, or the face of one's friend" (211). Cather's "something soft and wild and free" echoes Pater's something "exquisite," "strange," and "curious." Friendship is clearly implied, and that friendship is just as clearly homoerotic. For both Cather and Pater, male friendship is the "imaginative stimulus" (Pater, *Marius* 238) shaping their art.[9] That Pater deleted the conclusion from the second edition of *The Renaissance* suggests its erotic potential. As Reade points out, "It was not much. But whatever it was, it was a significant gesture in the Victorian moral continuum" (20).[10]

Cather's allusion to Pater is also a significant gesture in her appropriation of the homosexual literary tradition. In her final rendition of the Sacred Band, the values she associates with male friendship attain the spiritual truth Claude Wheeler glimpses at the end of *One of Ours*. If no longer in the physical presence of his friend and companion, the memory of Vaillant and their life together strengthens Latour's fortitude. His death-bed reverie once again recalls the moment in their native Auvergne when they anxiously awaited the diligence for Paris to carry them into the unknown. The earlier voyage resembles the one Latour is now making, and the face of his friend figures in both. In Pater's conclusion, as in Whitman's "When I Heard at the Close of the Day," the presence of the lover brings forth the soul. While her predecessors see the lover literally, Cather metaphorically extends their image. Unlike Godfrey St. Peter in *The Professor's House*, who relinquishes "something very precious," Latour connects with the "lover" and is released into something complete and great—a redemptive trinity of art, religion, and friendship.

Pater's "face of one's friend" illuminates a recurring vision in *Death Comes for the Archbishop;* indeed, the description of faces is a unifying pattern in Cather's design. Always sensitive to the shape of things, Latour is particularly sensitive to countenances, and while he does not seek miracles or faces appearing from afar, he finds the miraculous everywhere. All faces to him are revelatory— as Lee puts it, "to look closely is to understand" (276). By carefully reading either the face of old Sada or the cruciform tree, Latour experiences the "mysteries" and "holy joy" of religion (217).

This pattern builds to a supreme moment near the end of the novel when Latour, upon entering Santa Fe for the last time, looks upon the "golden face of his Cathedral" (271) set within the embracing arms of the Sandia Mountains. As David and Mary-Ann Stouck write, "The Bishop of the novel's title finds ultimate peace in the building and contemplation of his cathedral, in which religion and art are perfectly conjoined" ("Art and Religion" 294–95). For Latour, however, the cathedral and Father Joseph also unite as religious devotion mirrors dedication to one's friend. With its rising twin towers, the cathedral is as much a tribute to Vaillant as it is to the glory of God; a testament to art and religion, it is also the triumph of faith and friendship.[11]

In *Death Comes for the Archbishop* eroticism dissolves into spirituality in a process akin to the casting of the Spanish bell. Rather than spoiling the Angelus, exoticism enriches its tone; homoeroticism similarly enhances Cather's text. The mystery is that such a deeply religious book shows no hostility toward homosexuality, and it is the nature of this assimilation that helps make *Death Comes for the Archbishop* Cather's most perfect fiction, perfect in its fusion of theme and technique. Acknowledging Cather's achievement, E. K. Brown writes: "Her craftsmanship in language, her sense of a true economy, her command of rhythms individual without being eccentric, had never before reached such a delicate sureness" (257). Sexual aesthetics are part of this narrative strength. After the novel was widely read, many readers thought Cather herself was a Roman Catholic. Yet the narrative's authenticity demonstrates more than a depth of religious feeling. As James Woodress observes, "the novel was forged in the crucible of Cather's imagination" ("The Uses of Biography" 201)—a process that produced a profound humanity, including a sensitivity toward the friendship at the heart of her story.[12]

Particular friendship is Cather's crowning metaphor for "particular sympathy" (208). As Rosowski points out, "From the core friendship between Fathers Latour and Vaillant, a joyful mood extends outward, in what appears to be indiscriminate envelopment. . . . sympathy *is* the moral pattern" (VP 164). Homosexuality widens this metaphoric embrace and instills feelings in the novel that make Southern's assessment of *Spiritual Friendship* aptly descriptive of Cather's text: "The treatise that Aelred wrote on friendship is the most beautiful example of the casting of an ancient humanistic theme into a Christian mould" (35). Fusing the Greek ideal with Christian belief, Cather transmutes male friendship into a spiritual allegory. Like the fragrance of incense from the piñon fire, love between men gives *Death Comes for the Archbishop* the pervasive aura of a perpetual religious service; faith and friendship coalesce before us as the miracle of God's love appears in the face of one's friend. Consequently, *Death Comes for the Archbishop* is not only the apotheosis of the Sacred Band but the apotheosis as well of Cather's "thing not named."

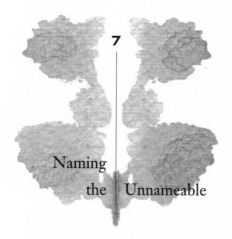

7

Naming the Unnameable

"WHEN we read Willa Cather's work creatively," urges Bernice Slote, "something like a web of living thought shimmers in the air between us, and around us, involving reader, book, and the writer herself" ("The Secret Web" 19). What happens to this shimmering, secret web when we attempt to name the unnameable in Cather's fiction? Does doing so provide a large enlightenment or produce instead a diminished mirage? Hermione Lee warns that "there is something reductive in trying to identify 'the thing not named,'" and she insists that it "*remains* unnameable—that is its point" (192). But while "the thing not named" does remain unnamed in Cather's texts, it is not unnameable by the reader. On the contrary, as Jo Ann Middleton points out, "Cather has always been experimental, challenging the reader to new modes of reading and to participation in the creation of art" (86). Naming the unnameable is the imaginative response to that challenge.

Throughout her critical statements, Cather returns to the idea that artists feel intensely and that art makes others feel. Her own art exhibits this passionate and irrepressible faith. Slote explains that "'feel' is Willa Cather's shorthand note for the living experience of art. As a pinprick can separate the living from the dead, so feeling is the simplest evidence of some reality created through the imagination. The absolute necessity in art is the personal encounter. The artist or the work of art succeeds if something works—if there is a response" ("First Principles" 46). Nowhere does Cather convey this belief more powerfully than in *One of Ours* when Claude Wheeler visits the Red Cross and talks with Mlle. de Courcy about the resiliency of the war-torn French people:

> "They must love their country so much, don't you think, when they endure such poverty to come back to it?" she said. "Even the old ones do not often complain about their dear things—their linen, and their china, and their beds. If they have the ground, and hope, all that they can make again. This war has taught us all how little the made things matter. Only the feeling matters."
>
> Exactly so; hadn't he been trying to say this ever since he was born? Hadn't he always known it, and hadn't it made life both bitter and sweet for him? (328–29)

Although Mlle. de Courcy articulates Cather's crucial idea, Claude intuitively feels its significance; the words may be new to him, but he fully understands their meaning. Here is Cather's characteristically self-reflexive art as the feelings evoked by a text determine its meaning and as readers, like fictional characters, participate in a "ceremony of creation" (Slote, "First Principles" 49). Here too is the connection between Cather's sexual aesthetics and the "novel démeublé" and the seamless fusion of feeling and form.[1]

Cather's treatment of homosexuality creates meaning in her texts by suggesting important aspects of her art, especially its potential for social commentary and its capacity for reader response. Although Alice Hall Petry cautions that the issue of homosexuality in Cather's fiction might possibly distance a reader from sympathetic involvement, Claude J. Summers argues that Cather's work enacts a redemptive drama in which readers can imaginatively participate. And while, as Slote says, "the subject of art must be humanity" ("First Principles" 47), the novel in particular has the ability, in Stephen Adams's words, "to speak to us intimately of the private worlds of other individuals" (12). The subject of homosexuality allows Cather to explore these ideals; her gay fiction informs her humanism, and a gay reading illuminates its value.

Homosexuality also becomes part of the incremental pattern central to Cather's creative process. Her treatment of homosexuality does not end with *Death Comes for the Archbishop* but continues to affirm human relationships in her later fiction. In Cather's short stories in *Obscure Destinies* (1932), male friendship settles like moonlight over the tranquil surface of "Two Friends," its sudden loss darkening the lives of her central characters; in "Neighbour Rosicky" male friendship becomes a bright metaphorical facet of a life "complete and beautiful" (71).[2] Sexual aesthetics also continue to evoke Cather's ambiguities as they do with her enigmatic German officer in *One of Ours*. For instance, while David Stouck argues that her last works show "affirmation of life through sympathy and understanding," ("Last Four Books" 300), homosexuality in *Lucy Gayheart* (1935) develops both affirmations *and* negations—what Susan J. Rosowski calls the Gothic undercurrents of Cather's "dark romanticism" (VP 204).

In addition to linking her male-centered novels of the 1920s, Cather's "thing not named" prepares readers for her female-centered texts that follow. Our uncertainty about certain characters' sexual orientation challenges the notion that Cather abandoned autonomous female characters and focused on men instead. The men Cather creates during the 1920s are not traditionally male, just as Alexandra Bergson and Ántonia Shimerda Cuzak are not conventionally female. Before writing about women in narrowing and constricting circumstances, such as Myra Henshawe in *My Mortal Enemy* (1926) and Sapphira Colbert in *Sapphira and the Slave Girl* (1940), Cather first wrote about men in contexts that redefined their manhood. As a result of this original focus, Cather's treatment of homosexuality in her male-centered novels charts the continued development of her art rather than its presumed decline and becomes a bridge between her early heroines and her subsequent feminism.[3]

Naming the unnameable also suggests ways in which Cather's texts anticipate some of the major gay fiction of the twentieth century. The 1930s was an explosive decade for gay literature in America—a time when, as James Levin observes, "the homosexual novel came into its own" (35). Surely Cather's male-centered novels of the 1920s helped pave the way from the repressive 1910s to the more expressive 1930s ahead, affiliating her elusive fiction with more sexually explicit texts like Blair Niles's *Strange Brother* (1931), Richard Meeker's *Better Angel* (1933), and Charles Henri Ford and Parker Tyler's *The Young and Evil* (1933).[4] By the end of the 1940s America's first "gay classics" emerged—all of which, it can be argued, owe some indebtedness to Cather's earlier novels. For instance, her friend Truman Capote's haunting *Other Voices, Other Rooms* (1948) lends itself to a comparison with Cather's evocative style, for as Levin avers, "the only thing clear about the novel is its ambiguity" (104). Gore Vidal's *The City and the Pillar* (1948), in which he claims to have been the first to write of a gay character as an all-American boy, is remarkably close to the feeling one has of *One of Ours.* And what has become one of America's preeminent gay novels, Christopher Isherwood's *A Single Man* (1964), bears more than a little resemblance to the complexities of *The Professor's House.*[5]

Descriptions of Cather's last fiction again confirm that homosexuality teased her imagination throughout her career. Edith Lewis recalls that Cather "had wanted for years to write an Avignon story. On her many journeys to the south of France, it was Avignon that left the deepest impression with her" (190). In the unfinished and unpublished novel "Hard Punishments," Cather follows a familiar narrative pattern. Friendship between two boys, André and Pierre, retraces Cather's fictional path, verifying Slote's observation that "Nothing in her work is unrelated to the whole" (Introduction ix). Exploring a recurring theme, Cather sets her story in France during the late Middle Ages. While Edith Lewis points out that "Willa Cather was greatly interested in the subject of blasphemy, as it was regarded in the 14th century" (quoted in Kates 201), John Boswell intriguingly connects homosexuality with medieval heresy:

> Gay people were also sometimes associated—to their manifest disadvantage—with the most despised of all minorities of the later Middle Ages, heretics. The push for conformity was nowhere more pronounced than in matters of faith, and the great theological discussions of the twelfth century had resulted by the mid-thirteenth in the establishment of rigid and exacting standards of faith to which all Christians must adhere or face the powers of the Inquisition, recently given to the order of Dominicans (whose severity in enforcing orthodoxy earned them the sobriquet 'domini canes,' 'the hounds of the Lord'). (CSTH 283)[6]

Placed within this context, "Hard Punishments" seems appropriately allegorical and a fitting coda to Cather's sexual aesthetics.

Consequently, a gay reading of Cather's fiction reveals more about the nature of her art than the nature of homosexuality. As an interpretative strategy, sexual aesthetics blend literature with literary theory and combine the pleasures of reading with critical ideologies. As a social critique, patterns of male friendship continue to question rigid gender categories and patriarchal assumptions. And while Cather and her work have been widely enlisted by scholars and critics, her treatment of homosexuality underscores her ongoing relevance to contemporary intellectual disciplines.

It is on another level, however, that Cather's gay fiction makes its deepest and most lasting impressions. If, for Cather, "Economics and art are strangers" ("Escapism" 27), then art is ultimately inimical to similar intrusions. Because her humanism steadies her focus on the fundamental realities of life and art, homosexuality enters Cather's canon less as a fact than as a feeling. Indeed, homosexuality partakes of the "eternal material of art" (Cather, "The Novel Démeublé" 40) and becomes an integral aspect of Cather's immense design, another glimpse of individuals caught in the complex behavior of living, and one of the few human stories repeating itself throughout history. That Cather evokes this particular story over and over again in her fiction recognizes its endurance; that readers continue to feel its presence further acknowledges Cather's own enduring achievement.

Notes

Chapter One · *"The Thing Not Named"*

1. Cather's treatment of homosexuality elicits diverse and often conflicting critical responses. For instance, while Faderman argues that "There is absolutely no suggestion of same-sex love in Cather's fiction" (*Surpassing* 201), Woodress points out both male and female same-sex relationships: "There are at least two friendships that come to mind immediately: the relationships between Marie Shabata and Alexandra Bergson in *O Pioneers!*, and Cherry Beamish and Gabrielle Longstreet in 'The Old Beauty.' And what is more, Cather treats these two friendships as admirable. At the same time, there are two overt examples of homosexuality that she treats very negatively in her fiction: the glimpse of the two American women who cause the accident in 'The Old Beauty' and the relationship between Clement Sebastian and James Mockford in *Lucy Gayheart* ("Cather and Her Friends" 84). Kaye adds a third example, arguing that the German sniper episode in *One of Ours* "recognizes homosexuality, even if it condemns it" (*Isolation* 188).

2. Concerning male homosexuality and literary style, Bawer asserts: "In the work of many a homosexual writer—from James and Proust to Oscar Wilde and Terence Rattigan—the author's homosexuality (latent or otherwise) is manifested not in the form of explicitly homosexual subject matter but in the form of certain qualities of style and

tone and perspective that suggest the distinctive, ironic position of a homosexual who is an esteemed member of a society that disdains homosexuality. Many such authors wrote portraits of society that are richly nuanced and elliptical, mainly because their situation made them all the more aware of nuances of language and gesture and because they were constantly having to talk around the truth about themselves. Denied their natural subject, moreover, many gay writers chose instead to concentrate on, and indeed to make a fetish of, style" (*A Place* 197).

3. Stout observes that "The 'reading' of textual silences, of what is not actually there but might have been there or is evoked by what is there, especially when writers call attention to the fact of such omissions, limitations, or outward pointings, is among the liveliest and most provocative developments in criticism in the past twenty years— and not in deconstructive criticism alone" (*Strategies* 2). Addressing Cather's "silences," Edward and Lillian Bloom write that Cather idealized "a form of literary reticence in which the hint or even the unspoken word convey the essential impression" and that "Compression and selectivity, insistence on total relevance . . . became Miss Cather's stylistic and thematic tenets" (*Gift of Sympathy* 188). What David Stouck calls "the art of ellipsis" ("Impressionist Novel" 60), Sergeant describes as simply a "gift of omission" (*Memoir* 194). And while Katherine Anne Porter asks if Cather's reserve is a "deliberate withholding" ("Critical Reflections" 146), feminist critics answer that Cather's "need to find a strategy of avoidance and suppression" was forced upon her by the double oppression of femaleness and lesbianism (Stout, *Strategies* 67).

4. See also Drake, *The Gay Canon*, esp. xv–xxii.

5. Stout supports this argument by observing that Cather "is able to use silences subversively to invite questioning of assurances that come too easily" (*Strategies* 68).

6. Cather's references to Thomas Mann alert readers to this duality. In her prefatory note to *Not Under Forty* she describes him as belonging to both the "backward" and the "forward-goers" (v), and in a longer essay in that volume, "Joseph and His Brothers," Cather remarks upon the "dreamy indefiniteness" (99) of Mann's fiction. Curiously, Heilbut notes that Mann's neighbor in California, Yalta Menuhin, responded differently to the novelist, "complain[ing] to her son that the Manns only discussed homosexuality. (She much preferred the

less graphic language of her favorite writer, Willa Cather, perhaps not realizing that Cather was a lesbian or that she had been deeply impressed by Mann's Joseph tetralogy)" (*Thomas Mann* 454). Heilbut writes that *Young Joseph* (1935) "deserves comparison with Proust's *Cities of the Plain* as a statement of the splendors and miseries of homosexual love" (549).

7. Similarly Donoghue writes that "'Something' is one of Pater's words for diaphaneity; it does not specify any object or quality, but it is still not nothing, it marks the site of a self-engendering"—"'Diaphaneity,'" Donoghue adds, "is an aesthete's word for freedom of mind and body" (*Walter Pater* 118).

Chapter Two • Gay Literary Traditions

1. Guy Reynolds points out that "Cather demonstrates the ability of art to create a 'hinterland' in which the creative intelligence fathoms problems given simplistic answers or avoided in other discourses. In her fiction she countenanced ideas, areas of American life and structures of human feeling overlooked in her journalism" (WCIC 24). In a striking parallel, David S. Reynolds writes that Whitman "often denounced certain kinds of behavior in his editorials and then sympathized with them in his poetry for purposes of cleansing or purgation. He did this with special frequency in the shrilly sympathetic poems of the 1860 edition, in which he lovingly embraces prostitutes, slave owners, and felons of all varieties" (*Whitman's America* 395).

2. Cather is not the only female to make male homosexuality central to her writing. Three other twentieth-century women writers are also notable for treating the subject with sensitivity and understanding: Marguerite Yourcenar, especially in her *Memoirs of Hadrian* (1951); Barbara Pym, whose novel *A Glass of Blessings* (1958) is excerpted in *The Penguin Book of Gay Short Stories* (1994); and Mary Renault, in her historical novels such as *The Persian Boy* (1972) and *The Last of the Wine* (1956). In fact, at least one critic has called Renault's *The Charioteer* (1953), set in Britain during World War II, both "a wonder of a novel" (Bawer, *A Place* 201) and "The best novel about male homosexuality" (196). An outstanding example from earlier in the century is *Despised and Rejected* (1918) by A. T. Fitzroy (pseudonym of Rose Laure Allatini), a novel of pacifism, war, and homosexuality—courageous for its time and therefore quickly banned and forgotten. Hammond further suggests that in the 1600s, Aphra Behn showed an inter-

est in "the attractiveness of sexual ambiguity in both men and women" and that her poetry "map[s] complex desires which do not make themselves easily accessible to the poet's or reader's understanding" (*Love between Men* 94–95).

3. On the relationship between Hadrian and Antinous, see Lambert, *Beloved and God*.

4. Stehling traces this medieval tradition of homosexual poetry back to the Carolingian poets of the ninth century, the North African poets of the sixth, and the late classical poet Ausonius. Describing its "sudden flourishing" during the twelfth century, Stehling writes: "Just as men were laying the foundations for universities, reviving interest in law and science, developing the tools of scholastic philosophy, and learning again to appreciate classical literature, so too were men writing poems of love and seduction among men or between older men and boys, as well as poetic defenses and condemnations of homosexuality" ("To Love" 151).

5. Sharp designates Shakespeare "the literary master of friendship" (*Friendship* 118)—a theme whose complexities are explored in *The Merchant of Venice* and *Romeo and Juliet*. Interestingly, it is Mercutio who elicits Cather's admiration of the "infinite wealth of [Shakespeare's] warm great heart" (Cather KA 389). Focusing on Shakespeare's sonnets, Pequigney moves beyond the "concept of 'Renaissance friendship'" toward an interpretation of Shakespeare's "erotic interplay between friends" (*Such Is* 65). See also Saslow, "Homosexuality"; Kleinberg, "*The Merchant*"; and Joseph A. Porter, "Marlowe."

6. On the structure of F. O. Matthiessen's *American Renaissance: Art and Expression in the Age of Emerson and Whitman*, see Bergman, *Gaiety*. Bergman states that "Structure is one way to make a point tacitly, and the structure of *American Renaissance* clearly argues for the supremacy of gay writers" (96).

7. While in *The Homosexual Tradition* Martin asserts Whitman's self-conscious homosexuality, Bergman argues that "Whitman's genius is not that he was able to establish a gay identity . . . but that he points out the difficulties so clearly. *Calamus* is ultimately a moving portrait of psychosexual isolation against which his grandiosity is clearly a strategy to prevent the most profound depression" (*Gaiety* 52).

8. Cather's ambivalence toward Whitman follows a gendered pattern of reader response. Miller observes that male poets like Ralph

Waldo Emerson, Henry David Thoreau, Sidney Lanier, and Algernon Swinburne all felt the need to both condone and condemn Whitman. In her male-identified phase, Cather too voiced conflicting opinions about Whitman. Yet, as Miller further points out, women writers such as Anne Gilchrist, Kate Chopin, and Muriel Rukeyser "turn to Whitman for the very element that the male writers would suppress" ("Poetic Progeny" 198): his "omnisexual vision" (190). The extent of Whitman's influence on Cather's mature work suggests that once she discarded her male identification, Cather affiliated herself more fully with Whitman, embracing either consciously or subconsciously his comprehensive theme.

9. Martin theorizes that "Whitman, like Melville, is suggesting that only when men accept their innate homosexuality can there be any hope for real change and a final victory over the aggression, acquisitiveness, and death-drive which, he believes, are rooted in heterosexuality. This is indeed a revolutionary idea; no wonder, then, that some critics have been so alarmed that they have been unable to address it" (HT 59).

10. David S. Reynolds writes that "Scattered reports of what was called 'sexual inversion' appeared in European medical journals through the 1870s and 1880s, but reports in America were scarce, and the word 'homosexual' was not used in English until 1892, the year of Whitman's death" (*Whitman's America* 396). By way of contrast, Schmidgall notes that "Several times, incidentally, Whitman used the word 'gay' in a way that makes one suspect it was already capable of carrying a 'homosexual' connotation at mid-century" (*Walt Whitman* xxiv)—an observation previously made in Shively, *Calamus Lovers* 23–24. Cory adds that "certainly by the nineteen-thirties it was the most common word in use among homosexuals themselves" (*Homosexual* 107).

11. For additional insight into Whitman's connection with nineteenth-century phrenology, see Lynch, "'Here Is Adhesiveness.'" As Lynch points out, many of the social and political reform movements of the nineteenth century had their basis in the science of phrenology. Part of this phrenological discourse stressed that "Friendship, not the family, is the foundation of social continuity" (71), and it is this belief that helped solidify Whitman's vision of an American democracy based on adhesiveness. In Lynch's view Whitman was a key figure in

the emergence of the modern homosexual role, "the social pattern of choosing same-sex companionship rather than an opposite-sex spouse as a basis for personal life" (92).

12. For a different reading see David S. Reynolds, *Whitman's America* 391–403. Rather than interpreting the sexual ambiguities of Whitman's poetry, Reynolds strains to keep Whitman in the genteel tradition, locating his erotically charged language in the nineteenth-century rhetoric of romantic friendship.

13. "That 'Greek' was synonymous with laissez-fare attitudes toward sexual behavior," observes Schmidgall, "is strongly suggested by Whitman's delight whenever *Leaves of Grass* was praised for its Greek spirit" (*Walt Whitman* xxv).

14. Cather's description of her 1902 tour of Ludlow and the Shropshire countryside was published in the *Nebraska State Journal* and is reprinted in WCIE 27–34. For specific details about Cather's meeting with A. E. Housman, see O'Brien, EV 250–51; Brown, *Willa Cather* 105–09; and Woodress, LL 158–59. Housman was on Cather's mind near the end of her life, when, as Woodress states, "She was going to write an article correcting all the misinformation that had gotten about regarding that episode in her life" (LL 503). Woodress speculates that the last letter Cather wrote was to Dorothy Canfield Fisher on 17 April 1947, asking for her friend's memories of their meeting with the poet (LL 529).

15. See Gervaud, "Willa Cather and France." Gervaud writes: "For some mysterious reason France and the French seem to have never disappointed [Cather] or hurt her feelings, whereas she was prompt to pass harsh judgments on her own country and fellow citizens" (65).

16. Cather's fondness for the work of Sir Richard Burton follows her interest in oriental styles and themes. Criticizing Burton's widow for destroying her husband's manuscript translation of *The Scented Garden*, Cather wrote in the *Nebraska State Journal*, 19 April 1896: "she placed the unquestioned home-and-fireside respectability of Richard Burton and wife above all the poetry of Persia. . . . Well, we have still some things to be thankful for. Sir Richard did succeed in publishing his matchless translation of those glorious Arabian romances, *The Thousand Nights and a Night*, that brought the strange sounds and color of the east into our tongue as Félicien David brought them into music" (repr. in Cather, KA 186). Interestingly, Burton—author, adventurer, and "pioneering sexologist"—attached to the 1885

translation of the *Arabian Nights* a "Terminal Essay" in which, according to Foster, he "provided information from many cultures and historical periods, paving the way for all future studies of the historical and cross-cultural aspects of homosexuality" ("The Annotated Burton" 92–93).

17. Boswell traces the English word *gay* to the Provençal word *gai*, which "was used in the thirteenth and fourteenth centuries in reference to courtly love and its literature and persists in Catalan—Provençal's closest living relative—as a designation for the 'art of poesy' ('gai saber'), for a 'lover' ('gaiol'), and for an openly homosexual person." Boswell adds that "The cult of courtly love was most popular in the south of France, an area noted for gay sexuality, and some troubadour poetry was explicitly homosexual" (CSTH 43).

18. Nordau writes that Paul Verlaine has "all the physical and mental marks of degeneration," signs visible in "his personal appearance, the history of his life, his intellect, his world of ideas and modes of expression" (*Degeneration* 119). Nordau is equally critical of Wilde and warns that "The ego-mania of decadentism" had its "English representative among the 'Aesthetes,' the chief of whom is Oscar Wilde" (317).

19. With regard to Loti's descriptive technique, "particularly as a creator of seascapes," Wake declares, "there can be no doubt that in this field he is a master with few equals" (*The Novels* 95).

20. Examining her letters, Woodress says that Cather once confessed "she would swoon with joy if anyone saw traces of Loti in her work" (LL 189). While the similarities between Cather and Loti, as well as between Cather and other writers mentioned in this study, are much broader than what I sometimes suggest, the scope of my argument considers only their connections with the subject of homosexuality.

21. In 1906, Xavier Mayne (pseudonym of Edward Irenaeus Prime-Stevenson) detected a "passional affection for young Yves on the part of the narrator going beyond mere friendship" and suggested that "a strong note of sexual relationship at times sounded in the tale" (*The Intersexes* 187). Wake supports this observation by noting that while Loti responded with differing degrees of intimacy to the handsome young men who served as prototypes for his characters, "Most of them were more than just friends and belonged to Loti's special category of *frères*, a term which Loti uses in his novels as well to designate close friendship" (*The Novels* 32).

22. Edel writes that Hendrik Andersen "inspired feelings in Henry James akin to love" (*Henry James* 498), an emotional intimacy that was passionately acted out in James's highly colored letters to the young sculptor. Likewise, Kaplan states that James "fell deeply in love" (*Henry James* 428) with Andersen, "whom he found as alluringly attractive as his work" (439).

Chapter Three · Intimations of Homosexuality

1. On the friendship between Cather and Stephen Tennant, see Hoare, *Serious Pleasures* 207–18 and "A Serious Pleasure." On Cather's relationship with Truman Capote, see Capote, *Music* 253–56. Another example of Cather's interest in unconventional men is her fondness for Charlie Chaplin. Yingling observes: "We cannot ignore, of course, the marvelous suspension of gender that occurs in Chaplin's films. If not gay, their main character often exhibits behaviors that make his gender identification ambiguous (he sews, he flutters his eyelashes, he blushes, is shy and practically defenseless)" (*Hart Crane* 245). This "suspension of gender," as Yingling argues, supports the possibility of a homosexual interpretation of Chaplin's films and may have influenced Cather's sympathetic response to the actor. See also Bohlke, *Willa Cather* 187.

2. While in *Gay Fictions* Summers dismantles the language of "Paul's Case," O'Brien in EV deconstructs its silences, suggesting that they reflect Paul's "muting by an oppressive culture and his increasing delight in nonverbal stimuli—music, perfumes, colors, food—as he regresses to the stage of human development prior to the acquisition of language" (307).

3. In "My First Novels" Cather herself responds to the critical hostility toward Nebraska as a fictional subject: "As everyone knows, Nebraska is distinctly déclassé as a literary background; its very name throws the delicately atuned [*sic*] critic into a clammy shiver of embarrassment. Kansas is almost as unpromising. Colorado, on the contrary, is considered quite possible. Wyoming really has some class, of its own kind, like well-cut riding breeches. But a New York critic voiced a very general opinion when he said: 'I simply don't care a damn what happens in Nebraska, no matter who writes about it'" (94).

4. The very act of writing *O Pioneers!* was itself a Whitmanesque gesture. Cather turns from the "studio picture" ("My First Novels" 91) of *Alexander's Bridge* (1912) to the freedom and openness of the

out-of-doors; her introductory poem, "Prairie Spring," written in Whitmanesque free verse, further underscores the unconventionality of *O Pioneers!*. "Instead of the sentence of fixed form, structure, and meaning," notes Martin, Whitman "offers a polymorphous field of pleasure and a political program that demands a reconsideration of the American dream and its potential" ("Whitman, Walt" 742). Artistically acknowledging this legacy, Cather anticipates later tributes to the poet, such as Hart Crane's "The Bridge" (1929), Federico García Lorca's "Ode to Walt Whitman" (1934), and Allen Ginsberg's "Howl" (1956).

5. Guy Reynolds writes that the West is "the land in which Americans discovered the 'Other'" (WCIC 63). Given this context, it seems even more appropriate that in writing *O Pioneers!* Cather would draw upon the homosexual literary tradition to emphasize her cultural plurality.

6. Early in the twentieth century, Edward Carpenter also theorized on the connection between human difference and creativity. In *Intermediate Types* he stressed that the homosexual "would be forced to *think*. His mind turned inwards on himself would be forced to tackle the problem of his own nature, and afterwards the problem of the world and of outer nature. He would become one of the first thinkers, dreamers, discoverers" (59).

7. In addition to Hellenizing *O Pioneers!*, a reference to "throwing the discus" also establishes parallels with Walter Pater, especially his *Greek Studies* (1895). Like Winckelmann before him, Pater looked to the ancient world for the highest expressions of human achievement, and for him, certain works of art—like Michelangelo's *David* or Myron's *Discobolus*—epitomized that perfection. Cather draws heavily upon his eroticized aesthetics in creating Emil, her "splendid figure of a boy" (77). Standing with his scythe, like Alexandra with her pitchfork, his sleeves rolled to his elbows, and a distant look in his eyes, he is statuesque, idealized, and mythic, resembling, except for his flannels and duck trousers, Pater's descriptions of ancient nude sculpture. By placing Emil in this rarefied atmosphere early in the novel, Cather justifies Carl's eulogy at the end, his praise of Emil as "the best there was" (305).

8. Cather's young Mexican guide reinforces this influence. Till now, much of the interest in Julio has focused on his importance to *The Song of the Lark* (1915) and "Coming, Aphrodite!" (1920). I would add that

he may also indicate Wilde's presence in Cather's mind at the time she was writing *O Pioneers!*, which would have been before, during, and after she met Julio in the spring of 1912. Cather's extravagant praise of her young friend's beauty, especially her reference to Antinous, conjures up images of Dorian Gray, who, also being posed in classical costumes, is likened to the idolized Greek youth. But in an even more striking parallel, Cather's letters not only envision Julio in New York, earning a living as an artist's model, but also express anxiety that artists would fight over him or that the affluent Mrs. Isabella Stuart Gardner would lure him away. Such fears echo (or parody) the opening chapters of *The Picture of Dorian Gray* (1891), where the artist Basil Hallward is expressing to Lord Henry Wotten a similar anxiety over the fate of his extraordinarily beautiful model. Here, perhaps, we can see Cather appropriating a gay text to shape her own writing, whether a letter or a novel. Furthermore, it is noteworthy that thoughts of Dorian Gray lingered in Cather's imagination. Although she had earlier stated, "We will have . . . no more such stories as *The Portrait* [*sic*] *of Dorian Gray*" (KA 389), similarities to Wilde's novel surface in Cather's "Consequences" (1915); and in the preface to the 1932 revised edition of *The Song of the Lark*, Cather once again invokes the novel's name.

9. The sympathetic tone of "Paul's Case" and *O Pioneers!* suggests that a broader cultural perspective on Wilde was taking shape after his death. Ellmann writes that even during his imprisonment, "The popular revulsion against Wilde's 'crimes' had begun to be checked by compassion" (*Oscar Wilde* 493).

10. Coincidentally, Wilde was accompanied to the State Penitentiary by George E. Woodberry, then professor of English at the University of Nebraska and later at Columbia University, the same George Woodberry who many years later introduced Cather to Amy Lowell when the two of them visited the poet at her Boston home.

11. There is in *O Pioneers!* an acceptance, right or wrong, of artistic and narrative identity as inevitable and as compelling as sexual desire. If, as Schmidgall argues, "The 1860 edition of *Leaves of Grass* is Whitman's *Dorian Gray*," in which "the dual theme of self-acceptance and self-assertion is climactically expressed" (*Walt Whitman* 319), then *O Pioneers!* is certainly Cather's "song of myself."

12. We can add Whitman to these affiliations. Wishing readers to accept his poetic spontaneity, Whitman declares that his catalogs are "Beautiful dripping fragments, the negligent list of one after another

as I happen to call them to me or think of them" ("Spontaneous Me," LG 103), which he arranges "at random in these songs" ("Our Old Feuillage," LG 175).

13. Russ enlarges this argument and views Cather's "nominally male characters," like Jim Burden, as "records not of male but of female experience, indeed of lesbian experience" ("To Write" 86)—males through whom, in their frustrated and unsuccessful love affairs with women, Russ believes Cather makes the poignant statement that "the desire for women, the love of women, is impossible to her protagonists" (83). Kaye offers a similar reading and asks, "What happens if we read *My Ántonia* as a lesbian novel?" (*Isolation* 98). By interpreting Jim Burden as a disguised lesbian, Kaye argues that *My Ántonia* would be "far more explicable and poignant," establishing as the center of the novel "Cather's inexpressible theme of the love of a woman for another woman" (106–07).

14. While Timothy Dow Adams argues that Jim and Ántonia are both imagined by Cather as homosexual and that "deep friendship based on mutual homosexuality was all they could ever share" ("My Gay Ántonia" 97), Irving interprets Ántonia's ethnicity as both displacing the theme of homosexuality in the novel and transposing Cather's ambivalence about her gender and sexuality: "the problems of Ántonia, her ostracization by the community for her various transgressive acts and style, are a metaphor for Cather's continued fear about what would happen if she were to announce her sexuality publicly and expose herself as female and hence, by definition, ineffectual" ("Displacing Homosexuality" 95).

15. Other Uranian journals include the *Chameleon* (with its Stevensonian subtitle *A Bazaar of Dangerous and Smiling Chances*)—whose one issue in December 1894 featured the story "The Priest and the Acolyte," written by John Francis Bloxam although often attributed to Oscar Wilde—and the similarly short-lived *The Quorum: A Magazine of Friendship*, which rearticulated Uranian themes as late as 1920. For a concise bibliography of English Uranian verse and its American counterparts, see Johansson, "Uranian Poets" 708–09.

16. Hammond points out that "much of the pederastic writing of the nineteenth century delights in imagining boys wounded or dead" (*Love between Men* 142). Such tropes, conflating grief with desire and longing with loss, prefigure the often intensely homoerotic poetry of World War I. Smith further observes that "In much of the Uranians'

verse, the synonym for 'adored boy' is 'Prince'" (*Love in Earnest* 193), the name given in *My Ántonia* to Lena Lingard's pet water spaniel.

17. A copy of Samuel Woodworth's "The Old Oaken Bucket" (1818) is among the items found in the tramp suicide's pocket in *My Ántonia*. Ravitch writes that "this poem well expresses a nostalgia for the country life and rural virtues that were steadily disappearing as industrialism spread and cities grew. It was frequently reproduced in schoolbooks and memorized. When set to music, it became the hit song of 1826 and remained popular for much of the nineteenth century" (*American Reader* 46).

Chapter Four · The Greek Ideal

1. In Plato's *Symposium* Phaedrus affirms the power of love to inspire noble principles and deeds: "And if there were only some way of contriving that a state or an army should be made up of lovers and their loves, they would be the very best governors of their own city, abstaining from all dishonor and emulating one another in honor; and when fighting at each other's side, although a mere handful, they would overcome the world. For what lover would not choose rather to be seen by all mankind than by his beloved, either when abandoning his post or throwing away his arms? He would be ready to die a thousand deaths rather than endure this. Or who would desert his beloved or fail him in the hour of danger? The veriest coward would become an inspired hero, equal to the bravest, at such a time; Love would inspire him. That courage which, as Homer says, the god breathes into the souls of some heroes, Love of his own nature infuses into the lover" (20).

2. Boswell writes that in the transfer of ancient learning, myth, and culture from the Greco-Roman world to the Christian world, "There is not much of a conceptual distance between the Sacred Band of Thebes and the *holy* pairs among the military martyrs of late antiquity, though it is a connection no previous writer has noted" (ssu 158–59). In my discussion of Cather's literary appropriation of the Sacred Band, I am suggesting a similar trajectory.

3. Griffiths provides additional support of Cather's artistic integrity: "At the moment when Dos Passos and his followers in the cult of experience were making the Great American novel something that a woman as noncombatant could never write, Cather reasserted the great tradition of war narrative as the province of artists more than of warriors. The literary models which she cites and employs in *One of*

Ours notably lack that firsthand experience which in 1922 was being proclaimed as necessary: the *Iliad*, the *Aeneid*, *Paradise Lost*, *War and Peace*, *The Red Badge of Courage*" ("Woman Warrior" 263).

4. For a discussion of Cather's spiritual quest, see Baker, "Before the Cruciform Tree." Baker argues that against the failure of evangelical institutions, "Cather posits an ideal of true faith, real compassion, and honest devotion—those ideals and values which she herself gave to her art and which she so devoutly admired in the truly faithful" (25).

5. While *The Homosexual Tradition in American Poetry* is a milestone in literary studies, Martin's candor also illustrates the value of gay criticism, especially its ability to enlighten so erudite a critic as Harold Bloom: "Why criticism has not addressed itself to the image of masturbation in Whitman, I scarcely know," Bloom ponders; "Richard Chase and Kenneth Burke noted it before me, and I have meditated upon it several times" (*Western Canon* 281).

6. This scene also asserts Cather's own autonomy as an artist by flouting the literary censorship campaign of the 1920s, spearheaded by Anthony Comstock and his New York Society for the Suppression of Vice. For a discussion of the effects of "the Comstocks" on the publishing history of "Coming, Aphrodite!" see Slote's introduction (ix–xxx) to Cather's *Uncle Valentine and Other Stories*.

7. Cather's frequent allusions to Plato indirectly position *One of Ours* within gay literary traditions. As Woods notes, "It is difficult to find an important text on male homosexuality, at least among those published before 1969, which does not refer to Plato's dialogues" (*Articulate Flesh* 96).

8. Henry James is even more rhapsodic than Fussell. Reviewing the regiments stationed at Aldershot in 1878, James calls them "the handsomest troops in the world" ("The British Soldier" 221). Seeing them pass on the streets in London, he notices in particular "their tight red jackets and tight blue trousers following the swelling lines of their manly shapes" (218). James's prose echoes an erotic fascination for the red-coated English soldier that is visible in places ranging from the novels of Jane Austen to the late Victorian homosexual subculture, where a sexual encounter with one of these uniformed men was known as "a bit of scarlet" (Gardiner, *Who's a Pretty Boy?* 24).

9. Martin argues that "Melville's fundamental orientation was homosexual but that he found no way of realizing that desire *on land*. Only in the world of the ship could he experience the free expression

of affection among men, and only in the 'primitive' cultures of the South Seas could he see a society that gave an honorable place to male friendship" (*Hero, Captain* 14). In *South-Sea Idyls* (1873) Charles Warren Stoddard also narrates a series of travel adventures in which he combines his sensual and spiritual responses to the tropical delights of Hawaii and Tahiti. With "No chart, no compass, no rudder, no exchange of references, no letter of introduction" (156), Stoddard luxuriates in "barbarian hospitality" (338). In a chapter titled "In a Transport" he rapturously describes an ideal of friendship in language suffused with homoerotic desire: "Twilight, fragrant and cool; a fruity flavor in the air, a flower-like tint in sea and sky, the ship's boat waiting to convey us shoreward. . . . O Thanaron, my Thanaron, with your arms about my neck, and B 's arms about you, and Nero clinging to his master's knees,—in fact, with everybody felicitating every other body, because it was such an evening as descends only upon the chosen places of the earth, and because, having completed our voyage in safety, we were all literally in a transport!" (322–23). For a fuller discussion of the connections between Stoddard's homoeroticism and his narrative strategies, see Austen, "Stoddard's Little Tricks"; see also Austen, *Genteel Pagan*.

10. Cather uses a metaphor of travel throughout her male-centered novels of the 1920s to develop her protagonists' spiritual quests: Claude Wheeler goes to France; Godfrey St. Peter visits Spain, France, and the Southwest; and in a variation of the technique, Jean Latour chooses to die in New Mexico rather than return to his homeland. Martin connects this narrative technique with gay fiction: "The theme of the Northerner discovering a land of warmth, beauty, and love is familiar, of course, and one that very often has homosexual meaning." Suggesting that this theme "is probably nowhere better expressed than in Mann's 'Death in Venice,'" Martin goes on to assert that "Mann was himself drawing upon von Platen, and one could equally well cite Lawrence, Forster, von Gloeden, Gide, and many others, all of whose works link the ancient gods and an older, darker civilization that remained in touch with the primitive sources of sensuality" ("Bayard Taylor's Valley" 15).

11. In centering Claude's self-persecution in the color of his hair, Cather anticipates A. E. Housman's posthumously published response to Oscar Wilde (qtd. in Laurence Housman, *My Brother* 226) that begins:

Oh who is that young sinner with the handcuffs on his wrists? And
    what has he been after that they groan and shake their fists?
And wherefore is he wearing such a conscience-stricken air?
Oh they're taking him to prison for the colour of his hair.

Laurence Housman explains that "though somewhat lacking in literary quality, [it] is so strong an expression of his feeling against social
injustice that I am sure he would have wished it to be known" (*My
Brother* 105).

12. See, for instance, Aristophanes' account of the origin of the
sexes and the pursuit of love in Plato, *Symposium* 33.

13. Embracing at the end of Xavier Mayne's *Imre: A Memorandum*,
its two central characters, Imre and Oswald, speak of "things grave and
gay": "We shall be all the happier now for what is real for us . . . I love
thee, as thou lovest me. I have found, as thou hast found, 'the friendship which is love, the love which is friendship.' . . . Come then, O
friend! O brother, to our rest! Thy heart on mine, thy soul with mine!
For us two it surely is . . . Rest!" (202–05). Of this novel Gifford writes:
"The story's ending is unprecedented—the first in American gay writing where homosexuals are united and happy as the tale closes" ("Stevenson, Edward Irenaeus Prime-" 687).

14. Another echo of Thomas Mann's *Death in Venice* (1912) occurs
in the final chapter of *One of Ours* with Cather's reference to the two
weeks Sergeant Hicks spent in Venice during the last year of the war.
"[I]f *Death in Venice* is," as Heilbut suggests, "Europe's first great homosexual story" (*Thomas Mann* 478), could *One of Ours*, given its range
of gay affinities, have a similar American distinction?

15. In recounting the Sacred Band's military performance at Chaeronea, Plutarch records that "when Philip, after the fight, took a view
of the slain, and came to the place where the three hundred that
fought his phalanx lay dead together, he wondered, and understanding
that it was the band of lovers, he shed tears and said: 'Perish any man
who suspects that these men either did or suffered anything that was
base'" ("Pelopidas" 155).

16. Other recent interpretations of this episode illustrate both its
ambiguity and the amount of critical attention it is beginning to
receive. Guy Reynolds argues that the scene is meant to distance
Claude from effeminacy: "He is allowed to have a 'sissy' name, but he
cannot be allowed to become a sissy'" (WCIC 117). Lee writes that "The

strange scene marks a denial—even, perhaps, a fear—of explicit homosexuality" (*Willa Cather* 181) and explains that Cather censors the sexual implications of the scene out of Claude's consciousness. Cramer
replies that "if Cather's use of the strange sniper scene is a conscious
attempt on her part to 'censor out the homoerotic possibilities,' then
it is quite obvious that Cather, too, recognizes the homosexuality of
her main character or else she would have had nothing to censor"
("Claude's Case" 148).

17. Woodress writes that "Cather buries in the last book of the
novel parallels between Claude and Parsifal and admitted to a cor-
respondent that she originally had intended to title this section 'The
Blameless Fool by Pity Enlightened'" (LL 328). Similarly, Wasserman
considers the "Blameless Fool" a "nice epitaph" for Paul in "Paul's
Case" ("Is Cather's Paul?" 128). It is interesting that both *One of Ours*
and "Paul's Case" can be linked to the Parsifal theme as a young man's
mythic search for beauty both conceals and reveals the literary tradition in which I am placing Cather's fiction.

18. Discussing the "rhetoric of idealism," Guy Reynolds points out
that Cather's use of free indirect discourse "blur[s] the line between
the narrating voice and the inner reflections of Claude" (WCIC 118).

19. For enthusiastic responses to Whitman's "gospel of comradeship," see Symonds, *Sexual Inversion* 189–90, and Carpenter, *Some
Friends.*

Chapter Five · Engendered Space

1. Perhaps the novel's strongest biblical echo concerning friendship
and the one most evocative of the ideals of the Sacred Band is John
15.13: "Greater love hath no man than this, that a man lay down his
life for his friends." Wild observes another biblical parallel and suggests that the New Testament story of Christ and Peter is an "emotional touchstone" to the relationship between Tom Outland and
Cather's professor ("'The Thing Not Named'" 273).

2. In an interesting correspondence, Martin discusses Whitman's
stylistic use of Dutch genre painting in "One Flitting Glimpse" and
the contribution it makes to his poetry: "It is a 'caught' moment,
viewed not directly but 'through an interstice,' thereby creating the
impression of real life observed, of the absence of art" (HT 79).

3. Discussing the "language of color" in *The Queen's Throat*, Koestenbaum suggests: "are there certain colors associated with homo-

sexuality? Blue: John Addington Symonds's *In the Key of Blue*, or Wilde's blue china. Green: Wilde's green carnation. Purple: purple prose" (52). "The links aren't exclusive or absolute," Koestenbaum cautions; "But even the wish to express oneself through color, to seek correlatives between one sense and another (synesthesia), to use color as code for other states, has been associated with nineteenth-century homoerotic culture" (52–53). Such possibilities open Cather's color symbolism to new interpretations. For instance, in 1915 Cather spent a week at Mesa Verde National Park near Mancos, Colorado, visiting the cliff-city ruins and gathering impressions she would later use in *The Professor's House*. In "Tom Outland's Story," however, "Mesa Verde" becomes "the Blue Mesa," a change that brings with it a multitude of associations.

4. Interestingly, the pine tree was the symbol for the Amory Art Show in 1913, a modernist representation continued by artists like Sidney Laufman and Charles Warren Eaton, "the pine-tree painter." Seen in this context, Cather's trees are symbolically closer to Frost's "Stopping by Woods on a Snowy Evening" than they are to Jewett's *The Country of the Pointed Firs*.

5. Pierre Loti is one of several sources for Cather's homoerotic fantasy. For instance, Hammond notes that "The idea that men might be able to inhabit an all-male world, an Eden without Eve, is a recurring dream in Shakespeare's plays" (*Love between Men* 58). Cather's scene also has a Stevensonian resemblance. Examining the textual interplay between homosexuality and male romances, Koestenbaum writes that "Though Robert Louis Stevenson was a unifying figure of his age, beloved by men of every political and aesthetic stripe, homosexual writers paid him special court" (DT 145). Highly praising Stevenson for his "boys' books," Cather describes him in the *Courier*, 2 November 1895, as "that great master of pure romance" (repr. in Cather, KA 232).

6. Although Boswell says that "There is no hint of sexual interest between the knights" (as CSTH 240) in the legend of Amis and Amile, Dellamora observes that "In retelling the tale, Pater emphasizes the specifically bodily aspect of the friendship" (*Masculine Desire* 150).

7. Connecting the life with the art, Donoghue writes that "Pater's paganism flourished upon the sight of beautiful men" (*Walter Pater* 100). This impulse is dramatically manifested in Pater's "Apollo in Picardy" (1893), another tantalizing analogue for *The Professor's House*.

8. Stockinger points out that "Even the earliest writers recognized a link between literature and sexuality that went deeper than the presence of erotic topoi" and thereby anticipated more modern theories of "the primacy of sexuality not only in the artistic process but also in the art product" ("Homotextuality" 137).

9. The "voyage perilous" is Cather's metaphor for artistic creation. In describing literary art, Cather wrote in the *Nebraska State Journal*, 1 March 1896: "To keep an idea living, intact, tinged with all its original feeling, its original mood, preserving in it all the ecstasy which attended its birth, to keep it so all the way from the brain to the hand and transfer it on paper a living thing with color, odor, sound, life all in it, that is what art means, that is the greatest of all the gifts of the gods. And that is the voyage perilous, and between those two ports more has been lost than all the yawning caverns of the sea have ever swallowed" (repr. in Cather, KA 417). Interestingly, Cather's metaphors of the "mighty craft" of art and "the voyage perilous" (KA 417) echo Whitman's conflated imagery of book, ship, and voyage, as Slote points out (see Cather, KA 351, n. 36).

10. E. M. Forster provides a similarly eroticized description of the genesis of *Maurice*. As he recalls in the novel's "Terminal Note," a visit to Edward Carpenter and his friend George Merrill made a profound impression upon him and kindled a creative spark, especially when Merrill touched his backside, "gently and just above the buttocks." "This sensation," Forster writes, "was unusual and I still remember it, as I remember the position of a long vanished tooth. It was as much psychological as physical. It seemed to go straight through the small of my back into my ideas, without involving my thoughts. If it really did this, it would have acted in strict accordance with Carpenter's yogified mysticism, and would prove that at that precise moment I had conceived." Upon returning to his lodgings, Forster immediately began *Maurice*: "No other of my books has started off in this way. The general plan, the three characters, the happy ending for two of them, all rushed into my pen. And the whole thing went through without a hitch" (249–50).

Chapter Six · Spiritual Friendship

1. Boswell adds: "The modern association of homosexuality with the arts had as its medieval counterpart a regular link with the religious life" ("Revolutions" 28).

2. Boswell concludes that "There can be little question that Aelred was gay and that his erotic attraction to men was a dominant force in his life" (as CSTH 222). Although celibate, Aelred was not antiphysical. For example, in *Spiritual Friendship* he attaches spiritual significance to a kiss on the mouth: "in a kiss two breaths meet, and are mingled, and are united. As a result, a certain sweetness of mind is born, which rouses and binds together the affection of those who embrace" (75).

3. Harmodius and Aristogiton are probably classical antiquity's most famous martyred pair. As Fone writes, they "were lovers and Greek national heroes, who died in defense of liberty. After their death, Athens named them guardians of Athenian liberty, their lives were taught in schools as exemplary, and at their shrine young lovers would pledge themselves to each other and to the ideals for which these two lovers fought and died" (*Hidden Heritage* 63).

4. Woods argues that "Of all the figures in the Christian pantheon, apart from Christ Himself, only Sebastian achieved the erotic status of so many boys and men in Greek myth [and] has in modern times taken on certain additional responsibilities in the area of male homosexuality"—"The ambiguity of his plight, and of his reaction to it makes Sebastian the ideal patron saint of the male, homosexual masochist" (*Articulate Flesh* 28–29).

5. "According to the chronology of the Christian faith," explains Woods, "God made Man . . . in His . . . image, and then made Christ in Man's image. So, given that my lover is made in God's image, shall I not find in him a trace of divinity? And, if God is made in my lover's image, shall I not quicken with desire for Him?" Woods continues: "This kind of unflawed reasoning lies behind a great body of devotional poetry most of it written by men, which is identical in its conventions to secular love poetry, and differs from it only in the name of the beloved: Jesus Christ" (*Articulate Flesh* 42).

6. Mayne supports this reading, adding that "Christ's personality and career; his vivid attraction to total strangers; the immediate spell that, right and left, he exercised on all men, so that they left everything for his sake; his magnetic charm over each human creature, young or old, who came within personal contact with him, are all traits of the mysterious powers of a noble and beautiful Uranian. . . . One may even ask whether the treason of Judas was the madness of a jealous homosexual passion, on the part of the betrayer; in a hatred of John, or of whomsoever else. We may also remember that Christ was a Jew, and

that his apostles were of an Oriental race inclined to homosexual passions" (*The Intersexes* 259–60). "The ideal Christ in omniscient sympathy," Mayne concludes, "must be profoundly acquainted with all human love" (260). In *De Profundis* Oscar Wilde similarly reflects upon the fact that Christ spoke in Greek: "It is a delight to me to think that as far as his conversation was concerned, Charmides might have listened to him, and Socrates reasoned with him, and Plato understood him" (87).

7. For an extended discussion of same-sex biblical pairs, including Jonathan and David, Ruth and Naomi, and Jesus and St. John, as well as "paired saints" such as Polyeucte and Nearchus, Perpetua and Felicitas, and Sergius and Bacchus, see Boswell, ssu, esp. chap. 4, "Views of the New Religion" (108–61).

8. On Julio's gender ambiguity see Flannigan, "Thea Kronborg's Vocal Transvestism." Examining Cather's letters to her friends, Flannigan argues that "Cather carefully avoids any description of Julio's *machismo*, and by comparing him to Antinous, the Emperor Hadrian's homosexual lover who drowned while crossing the Nile and who was later deified by Hadrian, suggests the image of a man who was sexually attractive to both men and women" (751).

9. E. F. Benson similarly encodes homoeroticism in his novel *The Inheritor* (1930). Attempting to define the Whitmanesque spell of a night spent out-of-doors with his friend, Benson's protagonist invokes language strikingly reminiscent of Cather and Pater: "I don't know what it was, but it was something primitive and wild and joyful" (49).

10. Pater restored a slightly revised conclusion to the third and subsequent editions of *The Renaissance* that includes the substitution of the word "colours" for "flowers." While possibly deflecting attention away from Baudelaire's *Les Fleurs du mal* (*The Flowers of Evil*, 1867), this change, I feel, further relates to Cather's passage, revealing similarities to Pater in symbolism ("blue and gold") in addition to those of rhythm and language. For fuller discussions of the revisions and publishing history of *The Renaissance*, see Donoghue, *Walter Pater* 65–69; Dowling, *Hellenism* 98–100; and Dellamora, *Masculine Desire* 147–48.

11. The cathedral towers function as another example of the "twinning imagery" running throughout *Death Comes for the Archbishop*. Rosowski writes: "Doubling is seen first in the central characters, Fathers Latour and Vaillant. Despite their different natures, the two priests seem as one, joined by twinning imagery: their similar clothing; their

common history, language, culture; their union in rituals of praying, eating, working; their two white mules" (*The Voyage Perilous* 166).

12. Woodress adds: "What Willa Cather needed to write the book was her gift of sympathy for the area and its people, her many visits to the Southwest, the long automobile rides she took with Tony Luhan, Mabel Dodge's Indian husband, who drove her to barely accessible villages in the Cimmaron Mountains, and the actual letters written by Father Macheboeuf about his and Jean Baptiste Lamy's work in the New Mexico diocese in the second half of the nineteenth century" ("The Uses of Biography" 201).

Chapter Seven · Naming the Unnameable

1. Details in the text of *One of Ours* heighten this remarkably telling scene. In Mlle. de Courcy's rooms Claude picks up a volume of *Reisebilder* (*Pictures of Travel*) by Heinrich Heine, "the most Whitmanesque of European romantic poets" (Schmidgall, *Walt Whitman* 229). The relaxed, almost meditative atmosphere is enhanced by the singing of Louis, the object of Claude's "erotic reverie" (Nelson 29). Claude associates the young man's "blond" voice with Nebraska's "summer wheat-fields, ripe and waving" (333). A wildflower also reminds him of home: "Claude found a group of tall, straggly plants with reddish stems and tiny white blossoms,—one of the evening primrose family, the *Gaura*, that grew along the clay banks of Lovely Creek, at home. He had never thought it very pretty, but he was pleased to find it here. He had supposed it was one of those nameless prairie flowers that grew on the prairie and nowhere else" (330). Reminiscent of Whitman's calamus plant, the poet's symbol for male love, Cather's botanical description evokes the contentment, connection, and erotic calm that Claude discovers in France.

2. The homosexual resonance of *Obscure Destinies* is strengthened by Cather's allusions to Thomas Gray, from whose "Elegy Written in a Country Churchyard" (1751) she took her title. According to Haggerty, Gray's homosexual sensibility was manifested in youthful romantic friendships with men—including Horace Walpole, a relationship that was broken off for reasons that have never been adequately explained—as well as in his poetry, where he memorializes the love he felt for other young men ("Gray, Thomas" 341). I am indebted to Timothy W. Bintrim for bringing these connections to my attention.

3. For a discussion of Cather's ambivalent feminism see Carlin, *Cather*. Of Cather's later, female-centered texts, Carlin writes that it is necessary "to acknowledge just how frustratingly feminist and potentially antifeminist they are simultaneously. Cather, one is forced to accept, will always demand to have her texts read both ways, and at once" (24).

4. According to Young, the 1930s "produced a number of novels about homosexuals that can be seen as the first 'gay novels' in the current sense" ("The Flower" 152). Other texts from this period include Reginald Underwood's *Bachelor's Hall* (1937) and Djuna Barnes's *Nightwood* (1936). Although published in the 1920s, D. H. Lawrence's *Women in Love* (1920) and *Aaron's Rod* (1922) are relevant here. As Hammond states, "Lawrence's creative engagement with his own homoerotic interests also led him to more positive ways of re-imagining masculinity" (*Love between Men* 187).

5. In addition to these connections, contemporary gay writers as diverse as Will Fellows (*Farm Boys: Lives of Gay Men from the Rural Midwest*, 1996) and Stan Persky (*Boyopolis: Sex and Politics in Gay Eastern Europe*, 1996) invoke the name of Willa Cather, and Cather's fiction is increasingly included in gay anthologies, such as *The Essential Gay Mystics* (1997) and *Pages Passed from Hand to Hand: The Hidden Tradition of Homosexual Literature in English from 1748 to 1914* (1997). But the most striking indication of Cather's place in gay literary studies can be found in Schmidgall's *Walt Whitman* (1997). A gay man writing the gay life of a gay poet cites Cather eight times, the first biographer of Whitman since Frederik Schyberg in the 1950s even to mention her. This, to me, speaks volumes about the subject at hand.

6. Boswell writes that "the late eleventh and early twelfth centuries were periods of 'openness' and tolerance in European society," while the thirteenth and fourteenth centuries were characterized by "restraining, contracting, protecting, limiting, and excluding" (CSTH 269–70). This historical overview suggests the setting for Cather's Avignon story, in which, as Kates summarizes it, one character is accused of stealing and is tortured by being strung up by his thumbs, and the other is punished for blasphemy by having his tongue torn out ("Unfinished Avignon Story" 200–02).

Works Cited

Adams, Stephen. *The Homosexual as Hero in Contemporary Fiction*. New York: Harper, 1980.

Adams, Timothy Dow. "My Gay Ántonia: The Politics of Willa Cather's Lesbianism." *Journal of Homosexuality* 12.3–4 (May 1986): 89–98.

Aelred of Rievaulx. *Spiritual Friendship*. Trans. Mary Eugenia Laker. Kalamazoo, Mich.: Cistercian, 1977.

Attwater, Donald, ed. *The Penguin Dictionary of Saints*. Baltimore: Penguin, 1965.

Austen, Roger. *Genteel Pagan: The Double Life of Charles Warren Stoddard*. Ed. John W. Crowley. Amherst: U of Massachusetts P, 1991.

———. *Playing the Game: The Homosexual Novel in America*. New York: Bobbs, 1977. Cited as PG.

———. "Stoddard's Little Tricks in *South-Sea Idyls*." *Journal of Homosexuality* 8.3–4 (spring–summer 1983): 73–81.

Bachelard, Gaston. *The Poetics of Space*. Trans. Maria Jolas. New York: Orion, 1964.

Baker, Bruce P., II. "Before the Cruciform Tree: The Failure of Evangelical Protestantism." *Literature and Belief*. Ed. John J. Murphy. Provo: Brigham Young University Center for the Study of Christian Values in Literature, 1988. 14–26.

Bawer, Bruce. *A Place at the Table: The Gay Individual in American Society.* New York: Poseidon, 1993.

Bell, Alice. "The Professor's Marriage." Murphy, *Willa Cather* 117–23.

Bennett, Mildred R. *The World of Willa Cather.* 1951. Lincoln: U of Nebraska P, 1961.

Benson, Arthur C. *Walter Pater.* New York: Macmillan, 1906.

Benson, E. F. *The Inheritor.* 1930. Brighton, Eng.: Millivres, 1992.

Bergman, David. *Gaiety Transfigured: Gay Self-Representation in American Literature.* Madison: U of Wisconsin P, 1991.

Blanch, Lesley. *Pierre Loti: The Legendary Romantic.* New York: Carroll, 1983.

Bloom, Edward A., and Lillian D. Bloom. *Willa Cather's Gift of Sympathy.* Carbondale: Southern Illinois UP, 1964.

Bloom, Harold. *The Western Canon: The Books and School of the Ages.* New York: Harcourt, 1994.

Bohlke, Brent L., ed. *Willa Cather in Person: Interviews, Speeches, and Letters.* Lincoln: U of Nebraska P, 1986.

Boswell, John. *Christianity, Social Tolerance, and Homosexuality: Gay People in Western Europe from the Beginning of the Christian Era to the Fourteenth Century.* Chicago: U of Chicago P, 1980. Cited as CSTH.

———. "Revolutions, Universals, and Sexual Categories." Duberman, Vicinus, and Chauncey 17–36.

———. *Same-Sex Unions in Premodern Europe.* New York: Villard, 1994. Cited as SSU.

Brown, E. K. *Willa Cather: A Critical Biography.* Completed by Leon Edel. New York: Knopf, 1953.

Bullough, Vern L. *Sexual Variance in Society and History.* New York: Wiley, 1976.

Capote, Truman. *Music for Chameleons.* New York: Random, 1980.

Carlin, Deborah. *Cather, Canon, and the Politics of Reading.* Amherst: U of Massachusetts P, 1992.

Carpenter, Edward. *Intermediate Types among Primitive Folk: A Study in Social Evolution.* New York: Kennerley, 1921.

———. *Some Friends of Walt Whitman: A Study in Sex-Psychology.* London: British Society for the Study of Sex Psychology, 1924.

Casey, Thomas M. "Mariology and Christology in *Death Comes for the Archbishop.*" *Willa Cather Pioneer Memorial Newsletter* 35 (fall 1991): 22–25.

Cather, Willa. "The Best Stories of Sarah Orne Jewett." Cather, *Willa Cather on Writing* 47–59.

———. "A Chance Meeting." Cather, *Not Under Forty* 3–42.

———. *Death Comes for the Archbishop.* 1927. New York: Vintage, 1971.

———. "Defoe's *The Fortunate Mistress.*" Cather, *Willa Cather on Writing* 75–88.

———. "Escapism." Cather, *Willa Cather on Writing* 18–29.

———. *The Kingdom of Art: Willa Cather's First Principles and Critical Statements, 1893–1896.* Ed. Bernice Slote. Lincoln: U of Nebraska P, 1966. Cited as KA.

———. Letters to Elizabeth Shepley Sergeant. Pierpont Morgan Library.

———. *My Ántonia.* Boston: Houghton, 1918.

———. "My First Novels [There Were Two]." Cather, *Willa Cather on Writing* 91–97.

———. *Not Under Forty: Studies of Literary Personalities and Certain Aspects of Literature.* New York: Knopf, 1936.

———. "The Novel Démeublé." Cather, *Not Under Forty* 43–51.

———. *Obscure Destinies.* 1930. New York: Vintage, 1974.

———. "On *Death Comes for the Archbishop.*" Cather, *Willa Cather on Writing* 3–13.

———. *One of Ours.* 1922. New York: Vintage, 1971.

———. "On *The Professor's House.*" Cather, *Willa Cather on Writing* 30–32.

———. *O Pioneers!* 1913. Boston: Houghton, 1962. Cited as OP.

———. *The Professor's House.* 1925. New York: Vintage, 1973. Cited as PH.

———. "Stephen Crane's *Wounds in the Rain.*" Cather, *Willa Cather on Writing* 67–74.

———. *The Troll Garden.* 1905. Ed. James Woodress. Lincoln: U of Nebraska P, 1983.

———. *Uncle Valentine and Other Stories: Willa Cather's Uncollected Short Fiction 1915–1929.* Ed. Bernice Slote. Lincoln: U of Nebraska P, 1973.

———. *Willa Cather in Europe: Her Own Story of the First Journey.* Intro. George N. Kates. New York: Knopf, 1956. Cited as WCIE.

———. *Willa Cather on Writing: Critical Studies on Writing as an Art.* New York: Knopf, 1949.

———. *Willa Cather's Collected Short Fiction, 1892–1912.* Ed. Virginia

Faulkner. Intro. Mildred R. Bennett. Lincoln: U of Nebraska P, 1965. Rev. ed. 1970. Cited as CSF.

————. *The World and the Parish: Willa Cather's Articles and Reviews 1893–1902.* Ed. William M. Curtin. 2 vols. Lincoln: U of Nebraska P, 1970. Cited as W&P.

————. *Youth and the Bright Medusa.* 1920. New York: Vintage, 1975. Cited as YBM.

Comeau, Paul. "*The Professor's House* and Anatole France." Murphy, *Critical Essays* 217–27.

Cooper, Emmanuel. *The Sexual Perspective: Homosexuality and Art in the Last 100 Years in the West.* 2nd ed. New York: Routledge, 1994.

Cooperman, Stanley. "The War Lover: Claude." Murphy, *Critical Essays* 169–76.

Cory, Donald Webster. *The Homosexual in America: A Subjective Approach.* New York: Greenberg, 1951.

Cramer, Timothy R. "Claude's Case: A Study of the Homosexual Temperament in Willa Cather's *One of Ours.*" *South Dakota Review* 31 (fall 1993): 147–60.

Crew, Louie. *The Gay Academic.* Palm Springs, Calif.: ETC, 1978.

Crew, Louie, and Rictor Norton. "The Homophobic Imagination: An Editorial." *College English* 36.6 (Nov. 1974): 274–76.

Crinkley, Richmond. *Walter Pater: Humanist.* Lexington: UP of Kentucky, 1970.

Crompton, Louis. *Byron and Greek Love: Homophobia in 19th-Century England.* Berkeley: U of California P, 1985.

Cruikshank, Margaret. *The Gay and Lesbian Liberation Movement.* New York: Routledge, 1992.

Dellamora, Richard. *Masculine Desire: The Sexual Politics of Victorian Aestheticism.* Chapel Hill: U of North Carolina P, 1990.

Donoghue, Denis. *Walter Pater: Lover of Strange Souls.* New York: Knopf, 1995.

Dowling, Linda. *Hellenism and Homosexuality in Victorian Oxford.* Ithaca: Cornell UP, 1994.

Drake, Robert. *The Gay Canon: Great Books Every Gay Man Should Read.* New York: Doubleday, 1998.

Duberman, Martin Bauml, Martha Vicinus, and George Chauncey Jr., eds. *Hidden From History: Reclaiming the Gay and Lesbian Past.* New York: New America, 1989.

Edel, Leon. "A Cave of One's Own." Murphy, *Critical Essays* 200–17.

———. *Henry James: A Life*. New York: Harper, 1985.

Ellmann, Richard. *Oscar Wilde*. New York: Knopf, 1988.

Faderman, Lillian. *Surpassing the Love of Men: Romantic Friendship and Love between Women from the Renaissance to the Present*. New York: Morrow, 1981.

Fetterley, Judith. "*My Ántonia*, Jim Burden, and the Dilemma of the Lesbian Writer." *Lesbian Texts and Contexts: Radical Revisions*. Ed. Karla Jay and Joanne Glasgow. New York: New York UP, 1990. 145–63.

Fiedler, Leslie A. *Love and Death in the American Novel*. New York: Criterion, 1960.

Flannigan, John H. "Thea Kronborg's Vocal Transvestism: Willa Cather and the 'Voz Contralto.'" *Modern Fiction Studies* 40.4 (winter 1994): 737–63.

Fone, Byrne R. S., ed. *Hidden Heritage: History and the Gay Imagination*. New York: Irvington, 1981. Cited as HH.

———. "This Other Eden: Arcadia and the Homosexual Imagination." *Journal of Homosexuality* 8.3–4 (spring–summer 1983): 13–34.

Forster, E. M. *Maurice*. New York: Norton, 1971.

Foster, Stephen W. "The Annotated Burton." Crew 92–103.

Fussell, Paul. *The Great War and Modern Memory*. New York: Oxford UP, 1975.

Gardiner, James. *Who's a Pretty Boy Then?: One Hundred and Fifty Years of Gay Life in Pictures*. New York: Serpent's Tail, 1997.

Gelfant, Blanch H. "'What Was It . . . ?': The Secret of Family Accord in *One of Ours*." Murphy, *Willa Cather* 85–102.

Gervaud, Michel. "Willa Cather and France: Elective Affinities." *The Art of Willa Cather*. Ed. Bernice Slote and Virginia Faulkner. Lincoln: U of Nebraska P, 1974. 65–83.

Gifford, James J. "Stevenson, Edward Irenaeus Prime-." Summers, *The Gay and Lesbian Literary Heritage* 686–87.

Green, Peter. "Sex and Classical Literature." *The Sexual Dimension of Literature*. Ed. Alan Bold. London: Vision, 1982. 19–48.

Griffiths, Frederick T. "The Woman Warrior: Willa Cather and *One of Ours*." *Women's Studies: An Interdisciplinary Journal* 11 (1984): 261–85.

Grumbach, Doris. "A Study of the Small Room in *The Professor's*

House." *Women's Studies: An Interdisciplinary Journal* 11 (1984): 327–45.

———. "Just William." Rev. of *Willa Cather: The Emerging Voice*, by Sharon O'Brien. *London Review of Books* 25 June 1987: 24–26.

Haggerty, George E. "Gray, Thomas." Summers, *The Gay and Lesbian Literary Heritage* 341–42.

Haller, Evelyn. "'Behind the Singer Tower': Willa Cather and Flaubert." *Modern Fiction Studies* 36 (spring 1990): 39–54.

Hammond, Paul. *Love between Men in English Literature*. New York: St. Martin's, 1996.

Heilbut, Anthony. *Thomas Mann: Eros and Literature*. New York: Knopf, 1996.

Hemingway, Ernest. *Ernest Hemingway, Selected Letters, 1917–1961*. Ed. Carlos Baker. New York: Scribner's, 1981.

Hoare, Philip. "A Serious Pleasure: The Friendship of Willa Cather and Stephen Tennant." *Willa Cather Pioneer Memorial Newsletter* 36 (summer 1992): 7–10.

———. *Serious Pleasures: The Life of Stephen Tennant*. London: Hamilton, 1990.

Housman, A. E. *A Shropshire Lad*. 1896. New York: Holt, 1922.

Housman, Laurence. *My Brother, A. E. Housman: Personal Recollections together with Thirty Hitherto Unpublished Poems*. New York: Scribner's, 1938.

Howlett, W. J. *Life of Bishop Machebeuf*. Ed. Thomas J. Steele and Ronald S. Brockway. 1908. Denver: Regis College, 1987.

Irving, Katrina. "Displacing Homosexuality: The Use of Ethnicity in Willa Cather's *My Ántonia*." *Modern Fiction Studies* 36 (spring 1990): 91–102.

Jacks, L. V. "The Classics and Willa Cather." *Prairie Schooner* 35 (winter 1961–62): 289–96.

Jackson, Graham. "The Theatre of Implications: Homosexuality in Drama." Young, *The Male Homosexual* 162–74.

James, Henry. "The British Soldier." *Lippincott's Magazine* 22 (Aug. 1878): 214–21.

———. *Letters [of] Henry James*. Vol. 4 (1895–1916). Ed. Leon Edel. Cambridge: Harvard UP, 1984. Cited as LHJ.

Johansson, Warren. "Uranian Poets." Summers, *The Gay and Lesbian Literary Heritage* 707–09.

Kaplan, Fred. *Henry James: The Imagination of Genius: A Biography.* New York: Morrow, 1992.

Kates, George N. "Willa Cather's Unfinished Avignon Story." *Five Stories.* By Cather. New York: Vintage, 1956. 175–214.

Kaye, Frances W. *Isolation and Masquerade: Willa Cather's Women.* New York: Lang, 1993.

Kazin, Alfred. *On Native Grounds: An Interpretation of Modern American Prose Literature.* New York: Reynolds, 1942.

Kellogg, Stuart, ed. "Introduction: The Uses of Homosexuality in Literature." *Journal of Homosexuality* 8.3–4 (spring–summer 1983): 1–12.

Kleinberg, Seymour. "*The Merchant of Venice:* The Homosexual as Anti-Semite in Nascent Capitalism." *Journal of Homosexuality* 8.3–4 (spring–summer 1983): 113–26.

Koestenbaum, Wayne. *Double Talk: The Erotics of Male Literary Collaboration.* New York: Routledge, 1989. Cited as DT.

———. *The Queen's Throat: Opera, Homosexuality, and the Mystery of Desire.* New York: Poseidon, 1993.

Lambert, Royston. *Beloved and God: The Story of Hadrian and Antinous.* London: Phoenix Giants, 1997.

Lee, Hermione. *Willa Cather: Double Lives.* New York: Pantheon, 1989.

Lell, Gordon V. "The Rape of Ganymede: Greek-Love Themes in Elizabethan Friendship Literature." Diss. U of Nebraska, 1970.

Levin, James. *The Gay Novel: The Male Homosexual Image in America.* New York: Irvington, 1983.

Lewis, Edith. *Willa Cather Living: A Personal Record.* New York: Knopf, 1953.

Loti, Pierre. *Mon frère Yves.* 1883. Trans. Mary P. Fletcher. London: Vizetelly, 1887.

Love, Glen A. "*The Professor's House:* Cather, Hemingway, and the Chastening of American Prose Style." *Western American Literature* 24 (Feb. 1990): 295–311.

Lynch, Michael. "'Here Is Adhesiveness': From Friendship to Homosexuality." *Victorian Studies* 29 (autumn 1985): 67–96.

Martin, Robert K. "Bayard Taylor's Valley of Bliss: Pastoral and the Search for Form." *Markham Review* 9 (fall 1979): 13–17.

———. "Edward Carpenter and the Double Structure of *Maurice.*" *Journal of Homosexuality* 8.3–4 (spring–summer 1983): 35–46.

————. "Whitman, Walt." Summers, *The Gay and Lesbian Literary Heritage* 736–42.

————. *Hero, Captain, and Stranger: Male Friendship, Social Critique, and Literary Form in the Sea Novels of Herman Melville*. Chapel Hill: U of North Carolina P, 1986.

————. *The Homosexual Tradition in American Poetry*. Austin: U of Texas P, 1979. Cited as HT.

————. "Knights-Errant and Gothic Seducers: The Representation of Male Friendship in Mid–Nineteenth-Century America." Duberman, Vicinus, and Chauncey 169–82.

Mayne, Xavier, ed. *Imre: A Memorandum*. 1906. New York: Arno, 1975.

————. *The Intersexes: A History of Similisexualism as a Problem in Social Life*. 1908. New York: Arno, 1975.

Meyers, Jeffrey. *Homosexuality and Literature, 1890–1930*. Montreal: McGill–Queen's UP, 1977.

Middleton, Jo Ann. *Willa Cather's Modernism: A Study of Style and Technique*. Rutherford, N.J.: Fairleigh Dickinson UP, 1990.

Miller, James E., Jr. "Whitman's Multitudinous Poetic Progeny: Particular and Puzzling Instances." *Walt Whitman: The Centennial Essays*. Ed. Ed Folsom. Iowa City: U of Iowa P, 1994.

Moon, Michael. "Disseminating Whitman." *South Atlantic Quarterly* 88.1 (winter 1989): 247–65.

Murphy, John J., ed. *Critical Essays on Willa Cather*. Boston: Hall, 1984.

————. "Willa Cather's Archbishop: A Western and Classical Perspective." Murphy, *Critical Essays* 258–65.

————, ed. *Willa Cather: Family, Community, and History (The BYU Symposium)*. Provo: Brigham Young University, Humanities Publications Center, 1990.

Nelson, Robert J. *Willa Cather and France: In Search of the Lost Language*. Chicago: U of Illinois P, 1988.

Nordau, Max. *Degeneration*. 1895. New York: Appleton, 1900.

Norton, Rictor. "Ganymede Raped: Gay Literature—The Critic as Censor." Young, *The Male Homosexual* 193–205.

————. *The Homosexual Literary Tradition: An Interpretation*. New York: Revisionist, 1974. Cited as HLT.

O'Brien, Sharon. "'The Thing Not Named': Willa Cather as a Lesbian Writer." *Signs: Journal of Women in Culture and Society* 9 (summer 1984): 576–99.

———. *Willa Cather: The Emerging Voice.* New York: Oxford UP, 1987. Cited as EV.

Pater, Walter. *Marius the Epicurean: His Sensations and Ideas.* 1885. Intro. Osbert Burdett. London: Dent, 1968.

———. *The Renaissance: Studies in Art and Poetry.* 1873. Intro. Lawrence Evans. Chicago: Academy, 1977. Cited as R.

———. *Studies in the History of the Renaissance.* London: Macmillan, 1873.

Pequigney, Joseph. *Such Is My Love: A Study of Shakespeare's Sonnets.* Chicago: U of Chicago P, 1985.

Perrie, Walter. "Homosexuality and Literature." *The Sexual Dimension in Literature.* Ed. Alan Bold. London: Vision, 1982. 163–82.

Petry, Alice Hall. "Harvey's Case: Notes on Cather's 'The Sculptor's Funeral.'" *South Dakota Review* 24 (autumn 1986): 108–16.

Plato. *Symposium.* Trans. Benjamin Jowett. New York: Macmillan, 1948.

Plutarch. "Pelopidas." *Plutarch's Lives: The Translation Called Dryden's.* Corrected and revised by A. H. Clough. Vol 2. London: Sampson Low, 1874.

Poggenbury, Helen Hunt. "The Dark Side of Loti's Exoticism: The Breton Novels." *French Literature Series* 13 (1986): 78–88.

Porter, Joseph A. "Marlowe, Shakespeare, and the Canonization of Heterosexuality." *South Atlantic Quarterly* 88.1 (winter 1989): 127–47.

Porter, Katherine Anne. "Critical Reflections on Willa Cather." Afterword. *The Troll Garden.* By Willa Cather. New York: New American Library, 1961. 139–51.

Ravitch, Diane, ed. *The American Reader: Words That Moved a Nation.* New York: Harper Collins, 1990.

Reade, Brian, ed. *Sexual Heretics: Male Homosexuality in English Literature from 1850 to 1900.* London: Routledge, 1970.

Reimer, James D. "Rereading American Literature from a Men's Studies Perspective: Some Implications." *The Making of Masculinities: The New Men's Studies.* Ed. Harry Brod. Boston: Allen, 1987. 289–99.

Reynolds, David S. *Walt Whitman's America: A Cultural Biography.* New York: Knopf, 1995.

Reynolds, Guy. *Willa Cather in Context: Progress, Race, Empire.* New York: St. Martin's, 1996. Cited as WCIC.

Rosenfels, Paul. *Homosexuality: The Psychology of the Creative Process.* Roslyn Heights, N.Y.: Libra, 1971.

Rosowski, Susan J. "Adaptations of *O Pioneers!* in the Classroom: Novel, Play, and Film." *Nebraska English Journal* 37.1 (fall 1991): 131–45.

———. *The Voyage Perilous: Willa Cather's Romanticism.* Lincoln: U of Nebraska P, 1986. Cited as VP.

———. "Willa Cather's Subverted Endings and Gendered Time." *Cather Studies* 1 (1990): 68–88.

Rubin, Larry. "The Homosexual Motif in Willa Cather's 'Paul's Case.'" *Studies in Short Fiction* 12 (spring 1975): 127–31.

Rule, Jane. *Lesbian Images.* Garden City, N.Y.: Doubleday, 1975.

Russ, Joanna. "To Write 'Like a Woman': Transformation of Identity in the Work of Willa Cather." *Journal of Homosexuality* 12.3–4 (May 1986): 77–87.

Ryder, Mary Ruth. *Willa Cather and Classical Myth: The Search for a New Parnassus.* Lewiston, N.Y.: Mellen, 1990.

Saslow, James M. "Homosexuality in the Renaissance: Behavior, Identity, and Artistic Expression." Duberman, Vicinus, and Chauncey 90–105.

Schmidgall, Gary. *Walt Whitman: A Gay Life.* New York: Dutton, 1997.

Schroeter, James, ed. *Willa Cather and Her Critics.* Ithaca: Cornell UP, 1967.

Sedgwick, Eve Kosofsky. *Between Men: English Literature and Male Homosocial Desire.* New York: Columbia UP, 1985. Cited as BM.

———. *Epistemology of the Closet.* Berkeley: U of California P, 1990. Cited as EC.

Sergeant, Elizabeth Shepley. *Willa Cather: A Memoir.* Philadelphia: Lippincott, 1953.

Sharp, Ronald A. *Friendship and Literature: Spirit and Form.* Durham: Duke UP, 1986.

Shively, Charley. *Calamus Lovers: Walt Whitman's Working Class Camerados.* San Francisco: Gay Sunshine, 1987.

Sinfield, Alan. *The Wilde Century: Effeminacy, Oscar Wilde and the Queer Moment.* New York: Columbia UP, 1994.

Skaggs, Merrill Maguire. *After the World Broke in Two: The Later Novels of Willa Cather.* Charlottesville: UP of Virginia, 1990.

Slote, Bernice. "Critical Statements: Literature." Cather, *The Kingdom of Art* 309–404.

———. Introduction. *April Twilights*. By Willa Cather. 1903. Lincoln: U of Nebraska P, 1962. v–xlv.

———. "First Principles: The Kingdom of Art." Cather, *The Kingdom of Art* 31–112.

———. "Willa Cather: The Secret Web." *Five Essays on Willa Cather: The Merrimack Symposium*. Ed. John J. Murphy. North Andover, Mass.: Merrimack College, 1974. 1–19.

Smith, Timothy d'Arch. *Love in Earnest: Some Notes on the Lives and Writings of English "Uranian" Poets from 1889 to 1910*. London: Routledge, 1970.

Southern, R. W. *Medieval Humanism and Other Studies*. New York: Harper, 1970.

Stehling, Thomas. "To Love a Medieval Boy." *Journal of Homosexuality* 8.3–4 (spring–summer 1983): 151–70.

Stockinger, Jacob. "Homotextuality: A Proposal." Crew 135–51.

Stoddard, Charles Warren. *South-Sea Idyls*. Boston: Osgood, 1873.

Stouck, David. "Willa Cather and the Impressionist Novel." Murphy, *Critical Essays* 48–66.

———. "Willa Cather's Last Four Books." Murphy, *Critical Essays* 290–304.

Stouck, David, and Mary-Ann Stouck. "Art and Religion in *Death Comes for the Archbishop*." *Arizona Quarterly* 29 (winter 1973): 283–302.

Stout, Janis P. *Strategies of Reticence: Silence and Meaning in the Works of Jane Austen, Willa Cather, Katherine Anne Porter, and Joan Didion*. Charlottesville: UP of Virginia, 1990.

Summers, Claude J. *Gay Fictions: Wilde to Stonewall: Studies in a Male Homosexual Literary Tradition*. New York: Continuum, Ungar, 1990.

———, ed. *The Gay and Lesbian Literary Heritage: A Reader's Companion to the Writers and Their Works, from Antiquity to the Present*. New York: Holt, 1995.

Symonds, John Addington. 1928. *Sexual Inversion*. New York: Bell, 1984.

Taylor, Bayard. *Joseph and His Friend: A Story of Pennsylvania*. New York: Putman's, 1870.

Thurin, Erik Ingvar. *The Humanization of Willa Cather: Classicism in an American Classic*. Lund, Swed.: Lund UP, 1990.

Wagenknecht, Edward. *Willa Cather.* New York: Continuum, 1994.

Wake, Clive. *The Novels of Pierre Loti.* The Hague: Mouton, 1974.

Wasserman, Loretta. "Is Cather's Paul a Case?" *Modern Fiction Studies* 36 (spring 1990): 121–29.

———. "The Lovely Storm: Sexual Initiation in Two Early Willa Cather Novels." *Studies in the Novel* 14 (winter 1982): 348–58.

Webb, Paul I., ed. *Blue Boys: Poems by Philebus, Edmund John, and Cuthbert Wright.* London: Gay Men's, 1990.

Whitman, Walt. *Complete Poetry and Selected Prose.* Ed. James E. Miller Jr. Boston: Houghton, Riverside, 1959. Cited as CP.

———. *Leaves of Grass.* Ed. Harold Blodgett and Scully Bradley. New York: Norton, 1965. Cited as LG.

Wild, Barbara. "'The Thing Not Named' in *The Professor's House.*" *Western American Literature* 12 (winter 1978): 263–74.

Wilde, Oscar. *De Profundis.* 1905. New York: Philosophical Library, 1960.

Woodress, James. "Cather and Her Friends." Murphy, *Critical Essays* 81–95.

———. "The Uses of Biography: The Case of Willa Cather." *Great Plains Quarterly* 2 (fall 1982): 195–203.

———. *Willa Cather: A Literary Life.* Lincoln: U of Nebraska P, 1987. Cited as LL.

———. *Willa Cather: Her Life and Art.* 1970. Lincoln: U of Nebraska P, 1975. Cited as LA.

Woods, Gregory. *Articulate Flesh: Male Homo-Eroticism and Modern Poetry.* New Haven: Yale UP, 1987.

Yingling, Thomas E. *Hart Crane and the Homosexual Text: New Thresholds, New Anatomies.* Chicago: U of Chicago P, 1990.

Young, Ian. "The Flower beneath the Foot: A Short History of the Gay Novel." Young, *The Male Homosexual* 149–61.

———, ed. *The Male Homosexual in Literature: A Bibliography.* Metuchen, N.J.: Scarecrow, 1975.

Index